The Little Black Bar Book
A Comprehensive Guide to Starting, Owning & Operating your own Bar or Nightclub

Chris Lenahan

This book or parts thereof may not be reproduced in any form, stored in a retrieval system or transmitted in any form by any means--- electronic, mechanical, photocopy, recording or otherwise----without prior written permission of the publisher, except as provided by United States of America copyright law.

Copyright © 2007 by Chris Lenahan
All Rights Reserved

Manufactured in the United States

Edited by Martin Stein
Designed by Darcy Kempton

International Standard Book Number: 143480545X (paperback)

CONTENTS

    Acknowledgements
    About the Author/ 1
    Introduction/ 4

BEWARE OF THE BEGINNING/ 12
    Bad Mojo/ 12
    Market research / 13
    Customer Profile/ 15
    Competition/ 17

CONCEPT DEVELOPMENT/ 22
    Concept Types/ 24
    Food/ 28
    Seasons/ 29

DEMOGRAPHICS/ 32
    Who are your Customers/ 32

LOCATION/35
    Location Options/36
    Lease Negotiation Tips/ 40

BAR DESIGN/42
    Flow/ 45
    Concept Ideas/ 46
    Entrance/ 47
    Bathrooms/ 48
    Seating/ 52
    Bar Areas/ 53
    Bar design & Layout/ 55
    Kitchen/ 61
    Storage/ 62
    Energy Points/ 65
    Décor/ 69
    Areas (VIP, Dance Floor, etc)/ 71
    Audio/ 77
    Video/ 84
    Lighting/ 85
    Attachment Points/ 93
    Equipment/ 99
    Cold Storage/ 100
    POS Systems/ 101
    Basic Equipment and Bar Items/ 102
    Speed and Service/ 103

THE BIRTH OF A NIGHTCLUB/ 105
    Summary/ 105
    Business Concept/ 105
    Legal and Administrative/ 106

STAFFING/ 111
How to Staff/ 112
Hiring a Bookkeeper/ 114

TRAINING/ 116
Upselling/ 117
Training Manuals/ 119
Security/ 120
Bartenders/ 122
Auxiliary Staff/ 123
Complaints/ 126
The Capture/ 127
Health and Safety Issues/ 128
Organization/ 129

THE CUSTOMER/ 130
Promoting Social Interaction/ 131
Instincts/ 132
Women/ 133
VIP's/ 134

MARKETING & PROMOTIONS/ 136
Promotions Team/ 136
Marketing Plan/ 136
Brand Marketing/ 139
Continued Promotions/ 140
Spending Habits/ 141
Promotions Calendar/ 144
Pricing Strategy/ 150
Price Wars/ 151

STEP BY STEP REFERENCE GUIDE/ 153
Critical Path Items/ 153
Timing/ 154

PROJECT STEPS/ 155
Business Plan/ 155
Market Research/ 155
Initial Budget/ 155
Business Plan to Raise Capital/ 156
Submit plan to Investors and Banks/ 156
Location Search/ 157
Find Attorney/ 158
Decide on a Location/ 158
Lease Agreement/ 158
Hiring Architects and Consultants/ 159
Concept design/ 159
Search for a Contractor/ 159
Contractor Bid's/ 161
Licenses/ 162
Bank Accounts and Payroll Accounts/ 163

  Drawings and your Contractor/ 163
  Landlord Hands Over the Venue/ 164
  Contractor Begins Work/ 164
  Signage/ 165
  Begin Advertising Campaign/ 165
  Hire GM and Key Staff/ 166
  Building Department/ 167
  Health Department/ 167
  Police and Local Alcohol Department Meetings/ 168
  Find Management Team/ 168
  Set up your Office/ 169
  Insurance/ 169
  Finding a Bookkeeper and Accountant/ 169
  Create Standard Operating Procedures/ 170
  Finalize Legal and License Requirements for Opening/ 170
  Source your Distributors and Suppliers/ 170
  Source Furniture and Bar Equipment/ 171
  Coke or Pepsi/ 172
  Merchandise/ 172
  Sound and Lighting/ 172
  POS Systems/ 173
  Recruit and Hire Staff/ 175
  Planning Opening Parties/ 175
  Training/ 176
  Press Releases/ 176
  Marketing/ 177
  Print Menus/ 177
  Equipment Installation and Goods Delivery/ 178
  Entertainment and Support Staff/ 178
  Order Liquor and Beer/ 178
  Construction Finals and Finishing Touches/ 179
  ATM/ 180
  Team Member Training/ 180
  License Approval/ 180
  Team Member Run Though/ 181
  Systems Testing/ 181

OPENING THE DOORS/ 182
  Friends and Family/ 182
  Local Press and Service Industry Management Professional's/ 182
  Service Industry Night/ 182
  The Day After/ 183
  Opening your Doors to the Public/ 183

BURN MONEY/ 184

FALLING INTO THE TRAP/ 185
  The 12 True Steps/ 185
  The 12 Deviant Steps/ 186

The Little Black Bar Book

ACKNOWLEDGMENTS

I would like to start by thanking GOD! Someone has to have been watching over me all these crazy years. Oh yeah The MOM too. Love you!

I would like to start with the entire Club Utopia crew for giving me my first big break, starting with Arin Brit may God rest his soul. Thanks for teaching me how to break down the barriers and just hug someone, Gino Lapinto, Robert Oleysick, Mike Fuller you pimp you still owe me half, and Pauly Freedman now a giant in the industry.

I would like to thank all of those in the Visual Magic crew who have worked so hard and long for so long you guys are still the best in the business. Keep on shining! Bret "I take longer than a girl to get ready" Doty my best friend, Danny Mills thanks for being the man behind the man. Harold "The Phantom Hillbilly" Wells, Doug Jablin, Carl "The lighting God" Hall keep on puffing, Zack the snack, Josh Camacho, Sterling, Therman, Leo Teo, Eric, Barbara, Karen and all the others who have been living the dream with me for over 11 years now.

- The Vegas Players

Steve D, Andy Masi, Ryan Doherty from 944 and Ratchet Magazine big thanks for helping me get the book to print. Richard Cheu, James Reyes, Scott Fisher, Tim Brennan, Chad Pallas from the Hard Rock, David "Don't paint the club white" Cohen, DJ Franky, Nick Popodopolis, Tony Verdugo, Robert Holt, Jimmy Foster, Jerome from RA, Robert Frey, Jeff Pollack, Jeff Beacher and Chad keep a leash on that goat, Josephine and Randi of CRI, Rico from the Rhino, David "the pimp webmaster" Phan, Darcy "hot wheels" Kempton and to the many others.

- The Phoenix Players

Ryan Jocque you're the man! Steve Cushner, Amy Cushner may God rest her soul. The lord always takes the good ones to be closest to him. Julien Wright glad you listened to me now, don't do any lounges. The Library Rock's! The entire Library crew Nick, Jay, Thomas Madgwick, Nas.

- The Bottom Line Group

Thanks to Jeff Pappas for being the glue and bumper and Nick Raymond for all the laughs.

For those who inspire me I can think of anyone greater than Scott Avjian who is a true Guru and a source of inspiration for all of those who are lucky enough to have worked with him. Thanks Scott.

Thanks Nicole for pushing me in the right direction. Don't miss the second book with all of those great tales! "Dirty Vegas"

When I space out and someone asks me what I am thinking about I will often think "I am just dreaming the dream"

Forgive me if I have spaced out and missed anyone you're all in my dream.

ABOUT THE AUTHOR

Chris Lenahan has been involved in developing, designing, and consulting for the highly competitive Bar/Nightclub industry since 1996! From his humble beginnings with his first company, VISUAL MAGIC (a company specializing in supplying Audio/Visual support and design), Mr. Lenahan has gone on to work with some of the country's largest and hottest Bars/Nightclubs, as well as the specialists and operators behind the scenes who have created these world famous venues.

With over a decade of first hand experience in designing, remodeling, consulting and building as well as installing sound, lighting and video systems in some of the largest night clubs /bars/theaters in the world, Chris Lenahan has become an international success story with numerous magazine and newspaper articles published about projects he has developed/designed and consulted on around the world. In 2001 he was featured in National Design Magazine for his work with the designer of Green Valley Ranch Hotel & Casino in Las Vegas.

Success was simply not enough for Chris, and by the year 2000 he took his intimate knowledge of the industry and began his first trek into bar/nightclub ownership with Freedom Nightclub (a 10,000 square foot nightclub specializing in world class international DJ's) in Tempe Arizona. In 2001 with the success of his first ownership venture, he expanded his interests becoming co-founder of the Library Bar and Grill, which was awarded "Bar of the Year 2001" by Bar and Nightclub Magazine. He has since held interest and ownership of several bars and nightclubs in Nashville TN and Scottsdale AZ.

His extensive experience in designing venues from scratch as well as new construction/renovations, venue selection, concept development, and market placement, and construction design/management have given him the insight to be able to design layouts that maximize flow patterns, design elements, and energy points needed for efficient and successful operations, as well as an understanding of standard City, County, and State Code requirements. He has also played a key role in hiring and training entire staffs for new concepts, as well as the marketing and promotional concepts and strategies for bar related entertainment venues, and the instituting of loss prevention systems to detect and prevent theft from staff members.

Playing such a critical role in designing new concepts and turning around failing venues has left him with the tools and knowledge for success, which he has recently passed on to the public by writing an informative 'how to book' on turn key bar and nightclub development and operations. His book is full of tales, insights, and information that is based on more than a decade of experience of working with the movers and shakers in the highly competitive bar and nightclub industry.

Chris Lenahan has also been doing business overseas in developing countries such as Vietnam and Thailand for over 5 years. He has owned and operated factories in Southeast Asia specializing in designer goods made and exported to the USA. His extensive experience setting up and doing business overseas as well as understanding the many fundamentals, laws, and guidelines associated with doing business in Asia have given him an understanding of the region, peoples, and cultures, including having acquired some of the local dialects needed for living and working in these developing countries with unlimited potential.

Noteworthy Bars/Nightclubs/Restaurant Clients

- **Club Utopia - Las Vegas NV & Scottsdale AZ**
- **Club RA - Luxor Hotel & Casino, Las Vegas NV**
- **Studio 54 - MGM Hotel & Casino, Las Vegas NV**
- **Baby's - Hard Rock Hotel & Casino, Las Vegas NV**
- **House of Blues - Mandalay Bay Hotel & Casino, Las Vegas NV**
- **House of Blues - Los Angeles CA**
- **C2K - Venetian Hotel & Casino, Las Vegas NV**
- **Venus - Venetian Hotel & Casino, Las Vegas NV**
- **RA – Luxor Hotel & Casino, Las Vegas NV**
- **Coyote Ugly - New York New York Hotel & Casino, Las Vegas NV**
- **Motown - New York New York Hotel & Casino, Las Vegas NV**
- **Light - Bellagio Hotel & Casino, Las Vegas NV**
- **Bikinis - Rio Hotel & Casino, Las Vegas NV**
- **Hush - Polo Towers Hotel & Casino, Las Vegas NV**
- **Vamp - Paris Hotel & Casino, Las Vegas NV**
- **Tequila Joe's - Imperial Palace Hotel & Casino, Las Vegas NV**

Introduction

- **Beacher's Rock House - Imperial Palace Hotel & Casino, Las Vegas**
- **Curve - Aladdin Hotel & Casino, Las Vegas NV**
- **Charo Showroom - Aladdin Hotel & Casino, Las Vegas NV**
- **Sevilla Showroom - Aladdin Hotel & Casino, Las Vegas NV**
- **Ovation Theater - Aladdin Hotel & Casino, Las Vegas NV**
- **Green Valley Ranch Hotel & Casino, Las Vegas**
- **SRO - Las Vegas NV**
- **Glow - Las Vegas NV**
- **Sapporo - Las Vegas NV**
- **Go Ventures - Los Angeles CA**
- **Club Rubber - Orange County CA**
- **IVAR - Los Angeles CA**
- **Pussy Cat Lounge - Scottsdale AZ**
- **CBNC - Scottsdale AZ**
- **Sanctuary - Scottsdale AZ**
- **Razor Magazine - Scottsdale AZ**
- **Library Bar & Grill - Tempe AZ**
- **Freedom - Tempe AZ**
- **On The Rocks - Nashville TN**
- **Gravity Lounge - Nashville TN**
- **White Party - NYC, NY**
- **G-Spot - Miami FL**
- **6 Lounge - Indianapolis IN**
- **De La Costa - Chicago IL**
- **Escape - Calgary Canada**
- **Acceleron Group - Las Vegas NV**

INTRODUCTION

I have been advised on many occasions that I should sugarcoat this book and put a happy face on the bar business. This would presumably lead to an increase in my own personal and financial gain. Some people believe that readers want to hear wonderful success stories filled with happy endings and inspirational tales. I believe that both success and failure come with a price, and that the cost of opening a bar can be paid in more than dollars. That cost may be friends, family, husbands and wives or even your life.

Inside this book, you will find stories and tales from my experiences regarding the highs and lows of the bar and nightclub business. My hope is to entertain and educate you with these tales, information, insights and humor.

My reasoning behind adding some of the darker stories is to honestly advise many would-be investors and owners about the realities of operating a bar or nightclub. It is not for everyone and can be the cause of much personal and financial hardship.

The very first interview should be done to yourself by yourself!

"So why is it that you want to open a bar or nightclub?" Your answer should start off with, "My dream has always been …" or, "I have always wanted to …" and if you have been in the business for years and understand the inner workings and pitfalls of being an operator, your answer should start with, "I am ready to …" or "I believe …".

I advise you now that bar and nightclub operation and ownership is not for everyone. But it is a great way to live your dream and make money doing so. Let your dreams begin!

Below is the cartoon strip "CAN'S" enjoy the Can's as they represent a parody of the owners, staff and patrons of the bar business.

Introduction

I would like to thank the sponsors of this book: Sallie Mae student loans and the Persian drug dealers from Los Angeles. Without both of these fine sponsors, this story would never have been possible.

In 1996, on a late, hot August night, I arrived in the land where millions of dollars are lost in mere moments entirely on games of chance. Glitz and glam gone wild, this was Las Vegas. The city is filled with a wild, transient mix of optimists, all chasing fantasies that end in as nightmares for most. Most are lucky if they are able to crawl home and just remember Vegas as a bad dream.

When I arrived in Vegas, I was scared, to say the least. I had no job, little money, and no idea of how to run a business. How was I to know that soon I would be on the inside of the largest bar and nightclub machine in the world? I would be working with true visionaries in the business, laboring and learning from some of the world's greatest and most talented bar and club owners.

Unless you have direct business relationships with these industry movers and shakers, you might never know who is behind these huge and complex operations. I have learned through trial and tribulation of the successes and failures in the largest and most successful bar and nightclub market in the world, where millions of dollars are made and lost.

I was fortunate enough to have worked with numerous creative minds through the years, learning the skills and knowledge that have carried me on to success in the bar and nightclub business.

With bar and nightclub failure being so common, I understand that anything which can help keep you in business is a good thing and that the most important tool for you to have is knowledge. I hope to pass on my insights and understandings of what it takes to create a successful concept.

How Did I Get into the Business in Vegas?

Portland, Oregon, 1996. I was in college and working full time to pay for school I had a dream, and that dream was to own my own business. I had almost nothing to start with. I was making $900 each month installing car stereos, plus I had my school loans each semester. With so little money to make my dream a reality, I can only tell you how hard work, luck and help from above made it possible.

I had a friend named Andy who worked in a factory assembling video projectors. Andy took me to his house and showed me one of the projectors in use. I was amazed to see the football game on his living-room wall. This was the coolest thing I had ever seen. Having always loved high-tech gadgets, I wanted one right away.

I bartered with Andy, and in exchange for some free work, along with some of my student loan money, I got my first video projector. I then sold the projector to another friend for double what I had bought it for. Then, I bought two more from Andy. My friend suggested I rent the projectors instead of selling them. He said, "Businesses and private parties will pay $300 to $400 per day for renting a video projector."

After calling around in the Yellow Pages, I found he was right. I was now in the audio-video rental business. My little company was born out of student loans, and a strong drive to succeed.

After selling one more projector, I sold one of the pair of projectors and used the money to buy two more for a total of three. Borrowing one from Andy brought the grand total to four, I then packed up my little Isuzu Amigo and moved to Las Vegas to make my fortune.

I arrived with no job and little money. I began by calling all of the equipment-rental places in Vegas and meeting with the managers to offer my equipment for lease. This didn't work too well and I made about $400 in the first two months. Things didn't look good until a family friend told me about a group of promoters who were holding a rave nearby.

I had never been to a rave, and didn't even know what one was! I soon came to find out that these popular and often illegal events are filled with thousands of underage kids dancing the night away in warehouses or secret desert locations hidden from the police. The larger raves are promoted by professional and well-organized groups and feature DJs and musical talent from around the world.

My First Gig

I met with the promoters, who agreed to pay me $1,500 to rent my projectors at the next rave. This was my first big break!

The event was a failure. I started the job I desperately needed armed with some metal poles and white bed sheets. It was held a 2 ½ hour-drive from Vegas out in the middle of the desert next to Area 51. What a sight! Half-frozen ravers and my bed sheet video screens blowing in the wind. When the temperatures fell into the low 40s, I didn't want to get out of the car to rewind the video tapes.

Introduction

Now that I look back on the whole event, it was lucky for me that not many people were around to witness my mess. Fortunately for me, some of the people who toughed it out gave some great reviews about the cool visuals. Thank God for good drugs!

The following week, I was back in Vegas where the same promoters had a Friday night event at a nightclub called Club Utopia. I went above and beyond what was expected of me so that the promoters of the Saturday night events would notice what a difference the visuals made. I was hired the next week by the club, starting at $400 every Saturday. Now I was making almost $4,000 a month working two days a week. I never dreamed of making that much money and I'd never been happier.

Club Utopia Las Vegas

This was where it all really started for me. What an experience! What an introduction to Vegas!

Utopia was my first large client in what would become a long list of huge names in the nightclub business.

Club Utopia was a cavernous mega-club, kept mostly in shadows as sweeping red lights blazed off the sweating walls. This dark dreamland had ghostlike figures in trances, swaying to heart-pounding music.

I have never used drugs and I don't drink. I couldn't figure out why the staff was so aloof and intent on keeping me out of the club's inner circle. I was in for a shock because, as it turned out, this was the main distribution point of ecstasy in the Las Vegas club scene. Persian drug dealers out of LA drove in thousands of tabs of ecstasy to my new job every week. Club Utopia was a safe zone made up of a tightly knit community, making it incredibly difficult for law enforcement agencies to penetrate.

I look back and it is easy to understand why everyone was so suspicious of me. I must have looked like an undercover agent, for sure. Drugs and alcohol have never bothered me and I found myself living vicariously through many of these people who were the rock stars of Vegas. The nightclub and bar business is a lifestyle, and that lifestyle has consumed many of my close friends and acquaintances.

With the huge success of Club Utopia came a seemingly endless supply of clients wanting to capture that something which made the place what is was. And make it part of *their* nightclub or bar. Through the years, I have traveled the U.S. and Canada, building bars and nightclubs, and always finding new ways to create that experience, always searching and perfecting the vibe, flow and function.

Here are a few names of clients over the years:

Club Utopia, Las Vegas, Phoenix
Studio 54, Las Vegas
Pussycat Lounge, Scottsdale
House of Blues, Las Vegas, Los Angeles
G-Spot Orlando
Sanctuary, Scottsdale
Go Ventures, Los Angeles
White Party, New York
6 Lounge & Restaurant, Indianapolis
Venus, Las Vegas
Axis/Radius, Scottsdale
Curve Las Vegas
Motown Café & Nightclub, Las Vegas
Green Valley Ranch, Las Vegas
Ovation, Las Vegas
Club Rubber, Orange County
Plush, Las Vegas
SRO, Las Vegas

Club Ra, Las Vegas
IVAR, Los Angeles
C2K, Las Vegas
Light, Las Vegas
Escape, Calgary Canada
Club CBNC, Scottsdale
Bigger, Los Angeles
Beacher's Rockhouse, Las Vegas
Coyote Ugly, Las Vegas
Sapporo, Las Vegas
De La Costa, IL Chicago
Baby's, Las Vegas
Bikinis, Las Vegas
Charo show, Las Vegas
Sevilla, Las Vegas "Charo Show"
Hush, Las Vegas
Razor magazine
Tequila Joe's, Las Vegas

Bars and nightclubs I have had an interest in:

Library Bar and Grill, Tempe
Pussycat Lounge, Scottsdale
Freedom Nightclub, Tempe
On the Rocks, Nashville
Gravity Lounge, Nashville

In Too Deep

After years in the business, I now find myself inside bars, nightclubs and now restaurants identifying shortcomings in the design or flow. I also find myself watching the bar as if I were a paid spotter looking for theft and inefficiency.

I can walk into venues and watch the volume of liquor and beer cross the bar and figure out how much the business is doing hourly and during peak and off-peak hours. I feel that I am cursed to never enjoy the patron experience as I cannot remove myself from the operations and creations aspects.

Introduction

I've amassed over 10 years of bar, nightclub and restaurant experience designing, consulting, owning and operating. I have never gone to school for design or architecture and have been forced to learn on the job and in the trenches.

My strength and experience allow me to produce turn-key operations from the initial design and concept development to marketing, training, staffing and day-to-day operations.

The feeling of walking into a bar and witnessing a massive failure of a concept is heartbreaking. I truly understand the pressures on people who have put up considerable sums of money and are locked into leases that might never need the option to renew.

After visiting a failing bar, I wonder if I could have saved that business from the failing management team, shortcomings of the design or layout or the blatant theft that has crippled the chances of it ever succeeding.

Las Vegas 1996

The bar and nightclub market only had about five real players in the marketplace: Club Rio, Club Utopia, the Shark Club, The Beach and the Drink. I had just entered the business and the competition was ugly, with dollar drinks and no cover or free drinks for ladies all night long. This was all around bad for everyone's business. It wasn't until 1998 that the club boom happened and venues were opening faster than the legs of a $20-a-dance stripper. Everyone believed that there weren't enough customers for all the clubs springing up, and that for everyone that opened, one would have to close.

Before anyone realized what was happening, Studio 54, Club Ra, C2K, Baby's and Light all entered the Vegas market in a flood of what I call "the endless summer nights." Champagne was falling from the ceilings like rain. Two-hour-long lines with $20 covers were normal, with some people dropping $100 to get in the doors quicker. Drugs, sex and alcohol ruled these long nights as patrons followed veterans from club to club to after-hours clubs until 11 a.m. the next day, and then on to a party in one of the mammoth hotels' suites.

During this time, the after-hours clubs were the places to let it all hang out. Club Utopia was the high-water mark of its time, followed by Drai's and the Spearmint Rhino Gentlemen's Club. After-hours were wild times. Large quantities of pills and cocaine were chased down by glasses of $500 champagne. This was heaven to all of us in the business. At the time, money was made by the basketful and hidden in shoe boxes.

Many of us in the industry thought it couldn't keep growing at this rate. Someone had to fold. Yet, the boom continued and the synergy of all of the new venues created new customers, offering up more and bigger and hipper venues. Somehow, lines stayed long and hot, sweaty dance floors kept pumping until the late-night hours.

The mass of clubs, bars and lounges finally did succeed in finishing off the weak operators, forcing the market to morph into a lounge/club scene: smaller-sized venues that are a mixture of nightclub and lounge, with lots of comfortable seating and VIP table service for high-rollers and hotel VIPs, this was the rise of the Ultra lounge.

The timing of the opening of all these venues and how it impacted the marketplace is a lesson I was lucky to live. The winners and losers were friends of mine. The ones who were willing to see the market and try to fit into what was needed were the ones who came out ahead.

Others who looked to professionals from other markets learned the hard way. The operators from outside markets came to Vegas thinking they could have the same success as they had enjoyed back home. They lost millions of dollars and were soon sent packing.

Meanwhile, the venues developed by the Light Group (Light, Caramel, Mist and Jet, as well as restaurants Stack and Fix) swept the local scene. The true mastermind behind the Light Group was Andy Massey, who went on to develop, operate and control Vegas' high-end nightlife venues for years to come. Massey's local experience in the market, starting with the House of Blues, allowed him to transform his knowledge and experience into a service industry empire.

Introduction

Alligator Joke

A guy walks into a bar with a pet alligator by his side. He puts the alligator up on the bar.

He turns to the astonished patrons and says, "I'll make you a deal. I'll open this alligator's mouth and place my genitals inside. Then the alligator will close his mouth for one minute. He will then open his mouth and I'll remove my genitals unscathed. In return for witnessing this spectacle, each of you will buy me a drink."

The crowd murmurs its approval. The man stands up on the bar, drops his trousers, and places his privates in the alligator's open mouth. The alligator closes its mouth as the crowd gasps. After a minute, the man grabs a beer bottle and raps the alligator hard on the top of its head. The alligator opens its mouth and the man removes his genitals unscathed as promised.

The crowd cheers and the first of his free drinks are delivered. The man stands up again and makes another offer: "I'll pay anyone $100 who's willing to give it a try."

A hush falls over the crowd.

After awhile, a hand goes up in the back of the bar and a woman timidly speaks up.

"I'll try, but you have to promise not to hit me on the head with a beer bottle."

Ok you have learned enough about me and my experiences now we will begin our journey into the bar business, on this road the first step's you will take will often be the hardest. Those steps include just putting the deal together and raising the capital to move forward.

Many of you with little or no experience in the business will be handicap by your lack of knowledge. This book will help guide you, teaching you some of the lingo and terminology that is used by industry insiders.

Partners, Landlords, Investors and soon to be employees are all going to want a leader who will take them to the promised land of a profitable high volume venue with a long term shelf life.

Remember a Leader leads from the front. So always stay calm and don't be afraid to ask questions.

Beware of the Beginning

New bars and nightclubs only get one shot at success. Every customer who comes through your doors is crucial to the success of your venue and you need them to have a great experience if you hope to have them return. It is vital that your venue is ready for success from day one.

Many bar and nightclub concepts fail within the first twelve months because they don't have an adequate plan in place.

There are many key factors that contribute to a Bar or Nightclub failing!

1- **Bad Management** – The most common problem is lack of experience in opening a new venue. Many managers come from concepts that have been up and running and successful. These managers have been working in an environment where all the operating procedures are already in place and functioning.

2- **Bad Owners** – One common failing is partners not Seeing Eye to eye about how the bar will be run. Often, money issues arise, with one or more partners unwilling to commit money to areas they feel are not effective. The most crucial areas are promotions and hiring and paying a good operations manager. It's not unusual for owners to think that because they have spent so much time in bars, it is easy to *run* a bar. At this point, I often find myself asking them if they should get their tax guy to run the bar and I will do their taxes for them! Owners and investors often need to step back and let experienced operators take over.

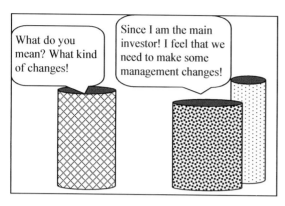 

3- **Underlining:** Under capitalization – Many venues begin without enough capital. During the construction phase, with all the delays and changes involved, the budget gets eaten up, leaving the concept little or no capital to properly execute promotions and operations. Many times, having a bad lease agreement and not allowing enough time for construction will drive a bar into a financial crisis before opening. Owners will find themselves paying rent while still in construction because of bad lease negotiations, construction delays and horrible city planning departments. Delays are inevitable, so add an additional 20% to the bottom line when figuring out your budget.

4- **Bad Partnerships** – Wow, I have fallen victim to this time and time again! Partnerships are often the best way to end up strangling someone who was your best friend six months ago. The level of stress in opening a new concept is often too much for many people, leaving them bitter and spiteful and more than one partner screwed over when all is said and done.

 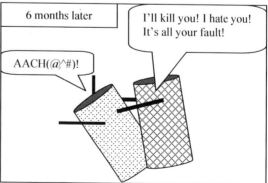

Bar Business Plan

If you need to raise money, a good business plan is in order. Many bars and nightclubs need large injections of capital in multiple phases from the very beginning. For construction costs or lease obligations, sometimes this amount will be in the millions of dollars.

I, for one, am not great at writing a solid business plan but I know many people who love nothing better than to raise capital for a dream in spiral-bound notebook form. I recommend you find one of the many templates available on the Internet.

Selling the dream to Investors

Many investors in the bar and nightclub business are often motivated not by ungodly returns but by the illusion of being young and cool again. They missed out on the good years, the chicks and the party life. Often, it was because of marriage or work commitments or just not ever being the cool guy. Now, they have some money and want to recreate the years they missed!

I like to say to these lost souls "The easiest way to make a small fortune is to start with a large fortune and then open a bar!" If you want to invest in a bar or club, great, but let professionals run the operation and stay out of the way! Have a good time with your friends and family, buying them drinks and partying in the VIP room all night. Just stay out of the way.

When you are trying to raise money for your bar or nightclub, selling this dream to investors is often 90 percent timing and 10 percent sales. Despite that, you usually will find the right person at the right time. Many people want to be a part of something exciting such as a bar or nightclub.

You need to make sure you present your business plan with legitimate goals and clear ideas of what you are trying to create. Make the potential investors comfortable with the risk vs. reward factor of a bar and nightclub.

Market Research & Analysis

I can't stress enough how important research is. You need to know if your dream of opening a bar or nightclub will actually work in the real world. You need to know what it is that your market and customers actually want.

There are four areas you should research:
1. Marketplace and customer base
2. Competition
3. Current industry trends
4. Seasonal effects on your business.

There are many professional market-research firms that can be contracted to do this for you. Successful companies specializing in market research include Market Decisions Corporation (MDC Research) and Moore Information, both companies are based in Portland, Oregon. They are experts in gathering information and opinions from targeted population samples. They can sit down with you, analyze your intentions and goals, isolate your target market and design appropriately worded questionnaires. This will enable you to gather honest and accurate information about what people will want and expect from your concept.

Where Do You Plan to Open Your Bar? Who is Your Customers?

This is the first question you need to ask. You are not going to want to open the wrong concept in the wrong location for the wrong demographic. It is important to get out and hit the local hot spots. Go out and do market research or hire a firm to send interviewers (or "interceptors") to all the bars and nightclubs frequented by your target demographic for a month or two. Ask people what they like and don't like about the existing venues, and what they think is missing in the realm of bars and nightclubs in your marketplace.

A QUICK CUSTOMER PROFILE

You may find that the promotions you thought were targeted to specific customer groups bring in patrons you didn't expect. Demographic overlaps are more common now than at any other time in history. Now, the rich and famous are rubbing shoulders with the masses in hot spots all over the country.

But it is still important to establish which customers you are trying to attract to your concept.
- **College students**
- **Twenty something**
- **Blue-collar workers**
- **The in-crowd/A-listers/celebrities**
- **Working professionals**

How Will You Do the Research?

This is going to require long nights of going from bar to bar and club to club, observing and meeting people asking customers and industry professional's questions. You want to find out what bars and nightclubs are popular, and what makes them so. What do their customers enjoy and what makes up their core group of patrons.

The Marketplace!

You will need to match your market needs to your concept in order to create a successful business. That doesn't mean you cannot open an Irish pub or a pool and darts bar in an upscale neighborhood. You just will have to adjust that concept to make your patrons feel comfortable in your environment.

Rock 'n' Roll Never Dies!

Here is a great example of marketplace changes based on trends from metropolitan areas on both the East and West coasts.

In South Beach, Vegas, LA and around the country, a wave of lounge-style rock 'n' roll bars appealing to a high-end, martini-sipping crowd have blossomed. Once upon a time, rock 'n' roll bars used to be for the American middle-class patron who enjoyed live music and cheap beer. Now, these rock 'n' roll bars have $20 cover charges, DJs and $16 vodka Red Bulls.

You never would have seen a line of BMWs or Benzs at these bars in the late 1990s. Now, these Rock Lounges hire expensive interior designers and invest millions on décor and rock memorabilia. You can see as times change so does the definition of what is cool.

Your target market patron and marketplace might not be able to handle or accept changes as fast as larger and more populous metropolitan areas, but this is often can be the high-risk, high-reward chance you must take if you want to be the first to offer the newest and coolest concept to your patrons. You will have to be the leader in your market!

You can draw a huge clientele to a new concept in your marketplace. But be sure you have your shit well thought out or you will be fucked! You must understand all of the parameters of a new concept, such as service, entertainment and music formats, and be able to execute those areas successfully.

Look at your marketplace demographics carefully! Can your potential patrons handle $10 to $12 martinis? Will your patrons be drinking three $12 martinis per night or can you get $4 for a beer and crank out volume? Or can your venue be a crossover concept, appealing to different demographics, so you have both types of patrons in your bar or nightclub

Local Competition

Once you are closer to deciding what type of bar or nightclub you want to open, you need to look at who is doing what and where with a venue similar to your dream.

- Are they successful?
- What are they doing right or wrong?
- How long have they been in business?
- Can you do as good as or better than them?

Once you have researched similar businesses, do you feel that these other bars or nightclubs will be your competition or will your dream be different enough that it can be located close to other similar venues and you still will be able to compete?

THE COMPETITION

"It is my belief that competition develops synergy!

"If I am wrong, then why do so many billion-dollar casinos open next to one another?"

Two Types of Competitors: Direct and Indirect

You need to take a good look at other local venues long before you lock in your location and concept. This is the time to study everything other venues and concepts are doing over your entire marketplace. What is working for other venues and concepts and what isn't? Do you feel the location you have chosen is the type of area you can jump into and provide a product on par with the other local establishments? Who are you competing against? Do you want to compete against another established concept? Is a similar concept 10 miles away going to affect yours?

Direct Competition vs. Synergistic Competition

Synergy is a very real effect that occurs in the bar and nightclub industry. As an intelligent operator, you are not going to open the same type of bar or nightclub next door to an existing one with the same concept. But with so many ideas to choose from, you will be able to find a twist on other local establishments.

I do not believe in competing with your neighbors since you all have the same goals. If you and your neighbors understand the business, they know that people today have extremely short attention spans and are always on the move. The typical customer will hang out for anywhere from 30 minutes to 2 ½ hours, depending on many factors, including seating, entertainment and the concept's popularity.

Thinking of other venues in your market as competitors is unwise. Think of them as promotional partners. Other local bars and nightclubs will advertise and promote their concepts, driving traffic into your vicinity for you or any other establishment to take advantage of. This is where you need to step up your promotions, driving those clients into your bar or nightclub, and becoming one of their stops on a long night of entertainment.

In entertainment districts, where there is a variety of different bars and nightclubs, you will find patrons who wander back and forth, looking for friends or simply barhop. I love this, as patrons feel obligated to buy a drink at each location and will often pay a cover charge each time, too.

In this situation. I like the synergy created by the area. People are restless and often will patronize two or three bars or clubs per night. Your dream is to become a must-hit location on the patrons' lists.

A direct competitor is one who is close to your establishment and is vying for the same clients with a similar concept. This is never a good situation and should be avoided at all costs (unless you are trying to drive this competitor out of business and have the capital available to do it). But even this is an incredibly bad business decision, as both businesses will need to cut each other's throats by reducing drink prices, running unrealistic promotions and charging little or no covers. Both venues end up losing.

Focus!
Your main focus should be on the bars and nightclubs within a 10-minute walk or five-minute drive from your location. Find out:
- The products and services they offer;
- Their competitive advantages in relation to your business;
- Their Pricing and how they promote their venue;
- Their Strengths and weaknesses;
- What could potentially threaten your business.

If You Have Another Competitor on the Same Street
Try communicating with them first ... if they are not already pissed at you for opening your bar next to theirs and want to throw you in the Dumpster. You might be able to turn the situation into something good for both. For example, if you both feature bands, your venues could alternate your music schedules, one hour on and one hour off. Or you

and the other bar could have a battle of the bands every weekend. Or have a mini Coachella festival that could last for three days and nights.

Indirect Competitors

An example of an indirect competitor would be a nightclub across town targeting a similar clientele base. Do not consider this competition, and focus on what you need to do and not what they are doing 10 miles away!

An indirect competitor is one that could possibly affect your business but is located farther than a 15-minute drive away. Why 15 minutes? Because a customer would have to make a serious commitment to drive that far while risking a DUI! Anything more than 15 minutes will be considered an inconvenience by a customer.

Don't even think of these other concepts as competition. Focus your attention on what is happening in your area, and try to promote your venue's growth and development.

Current Industry Trends

This country has been through many trends. Las Vegas has become a leader in nightlife trends, and you will find the rest of the country now follows Vegas. The big club boom of the electronic age has been massive. I was in the heart of it as a member of the Las Vegas' famous Club Utopia.

During this period, large-scale clubs popped up like toast all over the country, and house or electronic music was in, along with designer drugs such as Ecstasy. This was a true club drug and drove the market, along with the music, for years to come.

Music is often the driving force for changes in clubs, with popular culture following the music trends.

Hip-Hop and Pop Music

Look at the music trends only when building a nightclub. Hip-hop and pop music are huge for the nightclub industry. Hip-hop will always be good for clubs.

The new "Bling generation," with its imagery of sex; fast, flashy cars; and diamonds are all the rage! Just listening to a great hip-hop song makes everyone want to shake their booty.

House and Techno Music

House and techno have fallen by the wayside in recent years, with only the major metropolitan areas still able to support large house-only music clubs.

Rap Music

In the early 1980s to the late 1990s, rap was the revolutionary music for the masses. Its popularity and controversy still carry on today. But mixing rap with alcohol and drugs in an overcrowded nightclub may have a volatile effect!

Having been a part of many popular nightclubs targeted to the rap market, I have found that these clubs are often short-lived, with a history of violence and constant monitoring and harassment from local authorities.

Mash-Up

The latest popular trend in music is combining rock and hip-hop and rap to create a new sound. Top DJs who are able to create and perform this style are very popular now.

Gathering Information

If you need to gather good information on your marketplace, the best place to find it is in the bars and nightclubs themselves. The rumor mill in the industry is at work 24 hours a day, 7 days a week—plus overtime!

Who Are the Players to Look For in the Marketplace?

Unless you have direct business relationships with these industry movers and shakers, you might never know who is behind these operations.

STEVIE DAVIDOVICH: Pure Management Group's partner, marketing master and promotions guru, with an iron-fisted management approach and creative marketing skills. Stevie D. is a flamboyant character in any story.

ANDREW MASI: In the dictionary under "Workaholic Overachiever," you will find Andy's picture. The Light Group's Andy has a calm personality and boyish grin that reminds me of a fox before it eats the rabbit. Positioning people in key locations and a hands-on operations style make Andy the true omnipresent operator. His fanatic attention to every operations detail is truly a pleasure to behold.

JEFF PAPPAS: A behind-the-scene mover and shaker, Jeff is a restaurant consultant for the Acceleron Group. Watching Jeff work has been a humbling experience, with his quiet demeanor and stoic work ethic, Jeff has always reminded me of a storm that passes through in the middle of the night while everyone sleeps. Jeff has swept away the unneeded and unwanted, leaving a rainbow following his work wherever he has gone.

Promotions Companies and Promoters
These key people are great to know and you should pick their brains. They often will be the most helpful, as they know the inner workings of most of the local establishments and they will be able to give you the dirt on the scene.

Radio Personalities
These people are often dealing with live remote broadcasts at area bars and nightclubs. They can fill you in on what is hot. Remember, they also are making their living from business owners like you, doing promotions for a fee to the radio station or themselves.

Other Owners
It's hit-or-miss to talk to other bar and club owners, as they will not be happy to talk with someone they feel is a potential competitor. Tread lightly and be very diplomatic with them. Don't be surprised if some owners even try to get you to buy their business.

Local SIN Managers
Managers are a huge wild card in the business. When you find a good one, hold onto him tight and pay him well. These types of people are often hard to gauge.

They will be very helpful and good to know, as they will have a real understanding of the numbers and revenue streams from operating real-world venues located in the general area that you wish to open your venue. Listen to them. Don't be afraid to ask how much they or their bar make. Ask if they recommend any other managers or if there are any you should be warned about.

Bar Staff
If they are slammed, just sit back and watch them work. Look to see who is always busy and restocking or cleaning their area. These are the workers you want in your bar. Let them know you think they are doing a great job and that you are looking for good staff.

This also is where you might get information that you don't want to hear: the bar business' dirty laundry, such as which person does what drugs, sleeps with the staff or is a raging alcoholic. Take most of this with a grain of salt.

Remember, they are in the mix but not in the know, and often have third-hand information. I avoid the drama but it follows the bar industry like a tick on a blood hound.

CONCEPT DEVELOPMENT

con·cept (kŏn'sĕpt')
Noun.
1. A general idea derived or inferred from specific instances or occurrences.
2. Something formed in the mind; a thought or notion. See Synonyms at <u>idea</u>.
3. A scheme; a plan: *"began searching for an agency to handle a new restaurant concept" ADWEEK.*
The American Heritage® Dictionary of the English Language, Fourth Edition copyright ©2000 by <u>Houghton Mifflin Company</u>. Updated in 2003. Published by <u>Houghton Mifflin Company</u>. All rights reserved.

Developing your dream into a concept is the next step, now that you have researched your marketplace. You can mold your dream into a vision. You must create a name for your dream and then begin making notes on what it is you want. How do you want your dream to appear and appeal to others?

In lots of B and C markets,<<what are A, B and C markets?>> you have plenty of people opening bars and nightclubs without a clear vision or any concept development. They do not seem to care about the poor product they produce. They provide garbage to the public and then run it into the ground before moving on to the next venue. Not to worry, these soulless venues are often shit holes and don't last more than a year.

<u>Here Are Some Questions You Need to Ask About Your Concept</u>

- Who are you and what do you want your bar to represent?

Are you focused enough to operate the business, and enjoy what you have created, without neglecting your duties and responsibilities? Are you laid back and love music? Do you love the new wave electronic music scene with international DJs? Your bar should be a representation of what you enjoy!

- What Type of Lifestyle Is It That You Live?

Do you love sports and the thrill of competition? The beach bum life? How about partying all night and rubbing shoulders with the who's who in your city or town?

- What Is Your Dream of the Perfect Bar or Nightclub?

Concept Development

Have you always wanted to own the ultimate sports bar, with every game on a wall full of TVs? Have you always wanted to live on the beach and watch the sun go down with a cold margarita in your hand? You must pour your soul into creating this utopia.

- Where Do You Want Your Concept?

There is no limit to the locations where you can open a concept and succeed. Pushing the envelope in the bar and nightclub business is the norm!

Don't feel that you can't put a beach-themed bar up in the mountains. You need to think outside of the box, and give people what they want—and often what they don't expect. You could create the illusion of an eternal summer in the mountains.

Some of the country's hottest bars and nightclubs are in locations you would never expect. What about a country bar in the middle of LA or a sushi bar that turns into the hottest dance club in the city?

"Anything is possible and the possible can be anything!

- What Type of Food Do You Want to Serve?

A great beach-themed bar, to me, has got the hottest fish tacos and Mexican food in the city. You will sell buckets of cold beer and tequila shots to wash down all the spicy food. A great country-themed bar has oversized portions of everything, from the soda cups to the mountains of mashed potatoes and huge 1 ½-pound burgers.

- Can Your Patrons Afford to Come to Your Concept?

Look at your patrons' different levels of discretionary spending. You need to be sure your concept and your patrons' ability to splurge in a higher-end venue are a match. If you are a lounge looking to provide bottle service or expensive martinis as your specialty, you need to have patrons willing to spend $16 on a cocktail or $250 on a table.

Better to find out the areas your concept won't work before you invest huge amounts of money.

This Tells Me That I Must Be Drunk

A man walks into a bar and orders a shot. Then he looks into his shirt pocket and orders another shot. After he finishes, he looks into his shirt pocket again and orders another shot. The bartender is curious and asks him, "Every time you order a shot, you look in your shirt pocket. Why?" The man replies, "I have a picture of my wife in my pocket and when she starts to look good, I go home."

Concept types

Let's take a look at some of the different ideas available to you. Begin by choosing a concept and then molding it to fit your vision.

LOUNGES

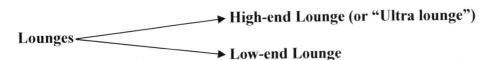

Examples of Ultra lounges are:
- Light, Bellagio, Las Vegas
- Tabú MGM Grand, Las Vegas

Low-end, rock 'n' roll or chill, ambient lounges represent this group. Examples of this type of lounge are:
- Snatch, Miami
- Bed, Miami
- Cherry, Calgary, Canada

NIGHTCLUBS

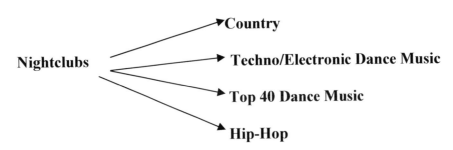

Country music dancehalls are some of the biggest nightclubs in the nation, with huge, hardwood dance floors, mechanical bull riding, country bands, DJs and free dance lessons. If you want a true Honky Tonk time, you will find it here. Examples of this type of club are:
 -Stampede, Calgary, Canada
 -Gilley's Dance Hall, Las Vegas

Techno/electronic dance music are the stages for internationally known DJs and electronic bands that were popular in the 1990s and are still hot all over Europe. Examples of this type of club are:
 -Crobar, Miami
 -Club Space Miami

Top 40 dance music is the format played at mainstream clubs. It consists mostly of hip-hop, R&B, pop, rock 'n' roll and electronic music. Examples of this type of club are:
 -Jet, Mirage, Las Vegas
 -Tao, Venetian, Las Vegas
 -Studio 54, MGM Grand, Las Vegas

Hip-Hop clubs are banging out new rap and hip-hop music, with DJs spinning scratching and mixing up to three records at once. Examples of this type of club are:
 -OPM, Caesars, Las Vegas
 -CBNC, Scottsdale

BARS

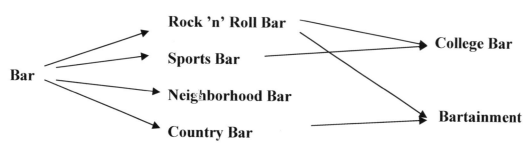

Rock 'n' roll bars are old-school bars with live music as the staple. They're making a huge comeback in the States and have always been popular in college towns. You can find local and sometimes national acts jamming out in these small, beer-chugging joints. Examples of this type of bar are:
 -Rainbow Bar & Grill, Los Angeles
 -Tin Roof, Nashville

Sports bars are a thriving section that has been picked apart now taken over by larger chains, resulting in mega sports bars. Almost every bar out there has a small portion of this concept integrated into it. Examples of this type of bar are:
- ESPN Zone
- Hooters
- Fox Sports Grill

Neighborhood bars are the stomping ground of hundreds of thousands and a second home for many patrons. These popular watering holes are surrounded by communities of loving and devoted customers who will make them their go-to spot for years on end. They were best depicted in the hit TV series, Cheers. Examples of this type of bar are:
- Cheer's TV
- Moe's Simpson's TV
- Slanted Clam Family Guy TV

Country bars are smaller than their full-sized dancehall cousins, but still wild and fun, filled with peanuts, beer and bikini bull riding. This concept should not be overlooked on your cool meter! The music and line-dancing make for hours of entertainment. Even with your "Achy Breaky Heart," you will find great friends and high times in "Low Places." Examples of this type of bar are:
- Tumbleweed Texas, Houston
- Cowboy Place, Chatsworth

College bars are places for higher learning, with subjects such as Beer Pong 101, Beer Chugging 103, not quite English 205 and Mom and Dad's Credit Card Economics 103. College students will study human anatomy until dawn, then sleep right through a physics test. This concept is timeless, and as long as you have a hot staff and cheap, cold beer, you will last as long as the university does. Examples of this type of bar are:
- Mill Avenue, Tempe
- 6th Street, Austin

Bartainment bars are a wave of theme-like bars with bartenders and cocktail staff in sexy outfits, dancing on stages or bar tops in choreographed routines. Just add cold beer, male hormones and hot chicks putting on a show, and you have created a good combination for selling lots of suds. Examples of this type of bar are:
- Hogs & Heifers, New York
- Coyote Ugly, New York New York, Las Vegas
- Library Bar & Grill, Tempe

PUBS

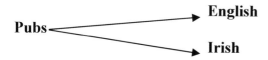

English pubs are based on a history of offering unique variety of high-quality draught ales. The experience of pitching down a pint or two of Guinness over the football game on the telly is a favorite pastime in England.

"The pub is more than just a shop where drinks are sold and consumed. For centuries, it has been a place where friends meet, colleagues 'talk shop' and business people negotiate deals; a place where people gather to celebrate, play games, or to seek quiet relaxation."
Quote from Pubs.com

Examples of this type of bar are:
 -The Pig and Whistle, worldwide
 -Cornwall's, Boston

Irish pubs provide a jolly, ole time, filled with fiddling bands, chipper barmaids and bartenders tossing dollar bills up to the ceiling.

"Irish pubs tell a story of Ireland's rich and celebrated pub culture. It is a culture of hospitable surroundings, good food and good drink, and friendly conversation."
Quote from Fado's website.

Examples of this type of bar are:
 -Fado Irish Pubs
 -Nine fine Irishmen, New York New York, Las Vegas

Crossover Concepts

You also can combine elements from one or more ideas to create a crossover concept that appeals to a wider demographic. For instance, you can integrate a diverse music format while maintaining exceptionally high levels of service but relaxing the restrictions on etiquette and dress code.

An example of a great crossover concept is a high-end rock 'n' roll lounge with a customer base ranging in age from 21 to 45, and making anywhere from $20,000 to $200,000 per year.

In such a venue, you'll have 30-year-old realtors showing up in their 6 Series BMWs, wearing $220 faded jeans and $55 T-shirts, buying $11 sour apple-tinis for 20-something college girls looking for a good time. Team members should be able to have Mohawks and tattoos but still make the best apple-tinis ever tasted. Female bartenders need to look good wearing combat boots, camouflage skirts and tank-tops. Your cocktail waitresses must be able to perform bottle and table service that rival five-star, white-glove restaurants.

But when you're done, look at the dynamic connections and different social and economic classes brought together!

The art of the crossover concept is always in the details. You will need to make sure that the service expected by higher-end patrons is met and exceeded on a nightly basis. Your concept must provide segmented areas for different groups to congregate and still be allowed to be removed from the regular public areas. An example is a raised seating area or a simple area of couches segregated with velvet ropes and manned by a host.

(I prefer to have the security team and hosts wearing bowling shirts with monogrammed names on the front and the concept's name and logo on the back.)

Anything can be turned into a crossover concept, but this should be done from the beginning and executed to your best ability. Turning an existing concept into a new crossover concept involves different dynamics that can only be dealt with on a per-case basis.

Food and Your Concept

The laws in some cities and states require the sale of food in order to obtain liquor and beer licenses. Often, just offering food and having a kitchen is good enough, but in some locales, restrictions mandate that a percentage of your sales be derived from food.

City and state offices will often audit your establishment at the one-year mark, giving you time to establish your business and/or upgrade your type of licensing to conform to your concept.

If you must serve food, there are ways to mitigate the costs. One is to find a limited partner to share the cost of the kitchen and food aspect, such as a local chef just starting out.\

You and your chef can then work together, or you can take a small profit from the food sales while sharing rent and utilities. You can be equity partners if you can find a happy medium for both parties.

In some markets food service is required for your Liquor License you can try the microwave and Hot Pocket trick, but this only works in some markets, and city and state regulators are wise to it.

If you are going to make a run at serving good food in a bar setting, here is a little advice: Do it big and do it right! Use lots of comfort foods, such as burgers, tacos and pizza. These are cheap, easy to make and hard to fuck up!

<u>Seasonal and Holiday Effects on Concepts</u>

Different types of seasonal effects can play a part in increasing or decreasing your business. Key factors such as adverse weather conditions and holidays contribute to varying levels of patronage.

Similar concepts in different temperate zones will feel the effects of seasonal changes differently. The need to understand that slow periods may occur throughout the year, and being able to prepare for these changes in advance, will mitigate the effects of these slow-downs.

The seasons are not all bad and big holidays will give a boost to your yearly revenues with good planning and promotion. Take advantage of the holiday spirit and plan an event to coincide!

- **New Year's Eve**
- **Labor Day**
- **Memorial Day weekend**
- **Halloween**
- **Independence Day**
- **St. Patrick's Day**

<u>Spring</u>

Spring is the beginning of the bar and nightclub season, bringing with it warmer weather and clear night skies as the winter weather resides. This is the optimal time to open a concept.

<u>Summer</u>

Summer can be slow for college bars. As school lets out for the summer, students return home and other activities, such as lake parties, concerts and sporting events, vie for their attention. In a college town, summer is the slow time. This is when you need to tighten the belt and run lean. Aggressively promote to locals and take this time to prepare for the next semester.

Summer for the rest of the country is a boom time as lines form outside of venues, with flocks of patrons enjoying the long, warm summer nights.

Summer for Resort or Vacation Location Oriented Bars
This is a great time for locations around the country. The weather is warm and the sun is out. This is the time for vacations and holidays. Bars in the costal regions will see a huge impact with beach-goers flocking to the costal towns. Summer in Miami is HOT!

Autumn
This is the time of year when holidays seem to fall every other weekend. The weather is still nice enough for female patrons to dress sexily and students fill the halls of college campuses again.

Winter
Winter weather can be good and bad. In areas hit by snow and freezing weather, you will have to pray to the weather gods to not ruin your weekends. In the southern most states, mild winter weather has little effect. <<good time for clubs in ski resort towns>>

As you approach Christmas, business will be considerably slower. Then there is a huge rush for New Year's Eve, only to see business fall off in January and February.

Budgeting for Future and Possible Concept Changes
How much of your profits will you reinvest into your bar or nightclub, and how? The success of a bar or nightclub is a long-term investment. For example, 10percent of your profits should be reinvested into future marketing campaigns and promotions.

The future is usually gloomy for most bars and nightclubs as the half-life of a good bar or pub can be anywhere from three to 15 years. The life of a nightclub or lounge will be considerably less, from one to three years.

Putting away money for the slow seasons and hard times is a good practice, along with knowing when to get out of the business or move on to the next concept while you are ahead.

Often, turning your present location into a new concept will work to rejuvenate the business, but this has its pros and cons.

- You are very familiar with the market.
- You have a bad reputation
- The venue has a bad reputation.

Concept Development

- You have a great lease.
- You know the perfect concept to put into place.
- You are under capitalized to execute the next concept.
- You don't truly understand the new concepts parameters.
- Your in a successful entertainment district
- Your Venue has specific space limitations.
- You own the building or plan on purchasing the building.
- You want to run another honeymoon period.

Honeymoon period= this refers to the first 6 months of your bar, which will be some of the busiest times of the existence of your bar.

Some Very Common Traits in Two Drunks

A man stumbles up to the only other patron in a bar and asks if he can buy him a drink.
"Why, of course," comes the reply.
The first man then asks: "Where are you from?"
"I'm from Ireland," replies the second man.
The first man responds: "You don't say, I'm from Ireland, too! Let's have another round to Ireland."
"Of course," replies the second man.
"I'm curious," the first man then asks: "Where in Ireland are you from?"
"Dublin," comes the reply.
"I can't believe it," says the first man. "I'm from Dublin, too! Let's have another drink to Dublin."
"Of course," replies the second man.
Curiosity again strikes and the first man asks, "What school did you go to?"
"Saint Mary's," replies the second man, "I graduated in '62."
"This is unbelievable!" the first man says. "I went to Saint Mary's and I graduated in '62, too!"
About that time in comes one of the regulars and sits down at the bar. "What's been going on?" he asks the bartender.

"Nothing much," replies the bartender. "The O'Kinly twins are drunk again."

Demographics

dem·o·graph·ic (dĕm'ə-grăf'ĭk, dē'mə-)
adj. also dem·o·graph·i·cal (-ĭ-kəl)
Of or relating to demography.
Noun.
A portion of a population, especially considered as consumers.

It is critical to research the demographics of your concept's core group of consumers. You need to know if the type of venue you wish to develop in a specific marketplace has the customer base willing to patronize and sustain your venue.

Customers need to escape and seek the new

Escape list	Seek
1-life	1-girlfriend/boyfriend
2-stress	2-New friends
3-reality	3-Good times/fun
4-lonleines	4-sex

Target Marketing

- Who are your customers?
- Where are your customers located?
- What do your customers enjoy?

Who Are Your Customers?
Let's put these into people into age-work categories:

- 21-26 College Students, Singles, Young Professionals.
- 26-30 Young Professionals, Working class.
- 30-36 Professionals, Working Class.
- 37-45 Professionals, Working Class.

As their age range gets higher, you can see that stability takes hold in their lives because of marriage, children or work-related concerns and responsibilities.

How many different nights can you expect these different categories to patronize a bar or nightclub? What type of broad-base consumer will your concept attract? What do they like and what are they looking for?

21-26 College Students, Singles, Young Professionals

This demographic wants to go out as much as possible. They make it a mission to go out up to four times a week. This group is highly energized by what is hip, new and popular with their peers. They will seek out and patronize different hot spots on multiple nights of the week.

This group is always looking for value in drink pricing and a low-to-no-cover charge on weekdays. On the weekend, however, they are willing to pay the cover charges large nightclubs demand.

College Students: Often frequent entertainment areas that are in close proximity to large campuses or education centers. This makes an ideal site to operate a bar.

Young Singles: Often prefer hip bars on good nights. Here they can meet and mingle with their peers and hunt for the opposite sex. They will dress nicer and have more disposable income than college students.

Young Professionals: Have the highest disposable income of this demographic group, often making close to $60,000 per year. Many professionals are developing earlier and younger, with high-paying careers such as mortgage brokering, real-estate, IT management or professional tradesmen. In Las Vegas, exotic dancers, valet attendants, bellman, waiters, cocktail waitresses and many other service industry-related professions can be in this group.

This group has money and will flaunt it by enjoying table and bottle service. They do not like to pay covers or wait in line as they spend good money and patronize venues regularly. These are big tippers!

A-Listers: I have left this group out but they are in every market. These are the professional bar- and nightclub-goers, traveling in groups, night after night, to all of the hot spots. They never wait in line and most likely have friends and acquaintances who work in the venues. This group will often be composed of service industry employees or aspiring entertainers, such as dancers, actors and musicians, or well-to-do spoiled socialites. They are known as "club kids."

Professional Athletes: Wow, what a group! Where do I start? From personal experience, I treat them like every other customer. They are great and will spend lots of money, but it is their friends who end up being the downfall of so many bars and nightclubs. I recommend you charge them and all of their friends cover and make them pay for their drinks as they make millions! I will offer them special seating arrangements and VIP room access but limit it to this.

__WARNING!__ The problem isn't the athlete but his tag-along friends!

Professional athletes are often accompanied by a group of friends and acquaintances that will use the athlete's fame and popularity in order to obtain VIP access and free drinks from bars and nightclubs.

The downfall occurs when the acquaintances develop relationships with your team members and are identified to the player. The acquaintances then will expect the same treatment when they are unaccompanied by the player and if they have developed a relationship with your staff they will likely receive it!

26-30 Young Professionals/Working Class

__Young professionals:__ This group is more mature than the previous group of young professionals and will often make runs to places like Vegas, New York, Miami and Los Angeles to party. They are likely to travel in small groups of three to five and prefer to have a booth or table in hot clubs and lounges. They still enjoy the bar scene, but the style and concept of bars and nightclubs they enjoy have evolved with their tastes.

This group has more disposable income than their younger counterparts and is willing to splurge to have a good experience.

The volume of unmarried and unattached professionals has grown in recent years to record levels as they enjoy the single life into their later years. This group has become more attached to achieving career goals and traveling.

__Working class:__ This fine group of die-hards enjoys the live music and good entertainment of the bar and pub scenes rather than the pounding club music and $16 vodka Red Bulls of nightclubs. They are often overlooked as they will wait in line, pay covers and buy drinks. This is more than can be said about the A- listers!

30-36 Professionals/Working Class

__Professionals:__ These patrons are still ready to throw down with the best of them and party all night. These are the lounge-going type or hip, new hot-spot creatures who can enjoy Monday night football games and beer as much as a martini and a strip club. This is the sushi and cocktail generation.

__Working Class:__ These are older more laid back, mostly married and divorced individuals, likely with children. They are a more cost-conscious group and more likely to hit the neighborhood bar or pub than the cool, hip nightclubs. These are your typical Hooters clientele and will love having lunch or an after-work drink in the local pub or bar before heading home. These patrons love to watch and cheer on their favorite teams so you should have a good audio-video system set up with lots of good, old rock 'n' roll, pop and even some hip-hop on the sound system.

37-45 Professionals/Working Class

<u>Professionals</u> These patrons are mostly out of the box for the lounge/club scene and are generally special-event customers only. They will occasionally hit the local pub or bar but prefer a more intimate piano lounge setting or restaurant bar over most other venues.

<u>Working Class</u> These football/baseball/basketball-loving monsters are the kings of the sports bars and will flock to watch big games and special events such as the Super Bowl, playoffs, March Madness and World Series games in your bar or pub. These patrons will enjoy pounding beers and eating hot wings and burgers for lunch or after work. Make sure you have hot waitresses as eye candy and they will keep coming back over and over.

Location, Location and Location

One of the most important and costly decisions is the selection of your location. There too many variables to list for every marketplace. All of these factors will be dependant on your total capital commitment to the project. How much money are you willing to invest in your concept to bring it to life? I will pay more for a good location as I would rather make ten percent of a million dollars a year than one hundred percent of nothing.

It is important to take your time and find the right location for your venue. This might take years but it will be worth it in the end.

<u>In choosing your location, you will have to factor in the following:</u>
- Leasing costs;
- Lease duration and extensions;
- New construction costs;
- Renovation costs;
- Other concepts in the immediate area;
- Traffic patterns, both foot and vehicle;
- Parking;
- Accessibility;
- Size in square footage;
- Quality of area (upscale, industrial, lower-income).

How Will You and Your Customers Benefit From Your Location?

Will your location be convenient for your patrons to find?

Is your concept near a freeway access point? This makes it convenient for patrons who travel from across town to get to you.

It is a good idea to make sure you look at all the possibilities of how your patrons will arrive and depart from your location.

Is your concept close to a large population center?

Think about how far your customer base will need to travel to get to your location, and if the customer base is conveniently located in your vicinity. The larger the population center, the more competition you will find in all of the demographic groups.

Does your location have easy and safe parking?

This should include a well-lit parking area, and if needed, you will have to provide a security patrol in the parking area for the safety of all of your patrons and staff. Parking is a great concern for many concepts, especially in metropolitan areas where patrons might be required to pay for parking. This can often discourage patrons who must search for parking. Cold weather and the winter make walking great distances unbearable and discouraging.

Why should they choose to go your bar instead of your competitors?

Location has a lot to do with the selection process of your customers. You need to ask yourself, after your research, what your customer has come to expect from other concepts in the area. Are patrons willing to sacrifice some convenience to find the hot spots? Can you offer a more convenient option to other concepts in the area?

Ask yourself how you are going to make the patron choose you and your concept over others in the area.

Location Options

Let's look at the different types of selections available for your concept placement. This will be one of your hardest decisions. Being in touch with your marketplace is critical.

- Destination Location
- Developed Area
- Developed Entertainment District

These three types of locations are what will be available to you. Choosing wisely is not good enough. Having a vision of the future and the changes taking place in your market are what truly matter. Experience, foresight and vision are what count.

Demographics

Let's take a look at the different types of location selections above and the pros and cons of each.

Destination Location

A destination location is best described as a concept off of the beaten path, away from other concepts, and usually in a stand-alone building. You will find that your local neighborhood bar is a good example of a destination location. Patrons must clearly make a conscious decision to travel to and patronize this particular venue.

- More initial promotions are needed to draw your crowd. You will need to invest more money up front for your advertising budget.
- Destination locations tend to have patrons stay longer.
- Your location to a major population center is within a 15 minute drive
- Parking in high-density population centers is limited.
- Walking in high-density population centers is possible.
- More locals and regulars are possible in a high-density center.
- Destination Locations tend to have lower rent and lease rates.
- You are in a higher-risk category, competing against developed bars.
- You better kick ass or patrons will not return.
- Well-lit parking patrolled by security is a must
- Your concept must have drawing and staying power.

Developed Area

Developed Areas are surrounded by commerce. They have a thriving consumer customer base coming and going. A developed Area can be considered to be any of the following:

1- Shopping Mall (indoor or outdoor)
2- Casino or Hotel
3- Strip Mall
4- Downtown or City Center
5- Shopping District
6- Sports Center

Let's take a closer look as to what you can expect from these sub-categories:
1- Shopping Mall (indoor or outdoor)
- High rent;
- Food is almost always mandatory;

- Foot traffic is great;
- Huge lunch rush and an early dinner crowd;
- Limited space/strict usage requirements from the mall;
- Trash and loading dock are usually far away.

2- **Casino or Hotel**
- Incredibly high rent;
- Lots of very strict guidelines;
- Lots of interaction and approvals needed;
- Traffic volume is incredible;
- A mutual working relationship and promotional piggy-backing;
- Competing directly with the casino patrons' gaming time;
- Casinos like for their patrons to find every good and service on site and you are one of those;
- -Your location inside the casino is also important. How far away is the parking and valet?
- -Working out a comp policy with the hotel or casino is important;
- -Work out a VIP policy with the hotel or casino for line passes and comp drinks for guests and staff.

3- **Strip Mall**
- Medium rent range;
- Good for bar or pub style concepts;
- Live music works well;
- Late-night parking is fantastic and well-lit;
- Bar-style food is a must, with good lunch specials;
- Live entertainment and sports work well;
- Lots of traffic so you can advertise on the front of your venue's windows;
- Easy delivery of supplies.

4- **Downtown or City Center**
- Rents vary greatly;
- High daytime and weekend traffic;
- Great lunch opportunities;
- Parking issues such as paid parking become a hassle;
- Patrons are professionals and will often need to hold meetings;
- After 5 p.m., can become a ghost town in some markets;
- Creating a safe environment for patrons is important after dark.

5- Shopping District
- More prevalent in Asia and Europe;
- Districts such as the Champs-Elysées in Paris or the night market areas in Taipei;
- High rents;
- The traffic both day and night is massive;
- Most traffic is foot traffic and parking is a nightmare;
- Patrons have expendable cash and are usually shopping or socializing.

6- Sports Center
- High to medium rents;
- High traffic on event days
- Convention possibilities;
- If your sports center team wins a game, this will drive sales;
- Team devotion and quality pre- and after-game parties are key;
- Patrons come early but leave immediately following the game;
- Good food is a must.

Female Hormones in Beer

Yesterday, scientists in the United States revealed that beer contains small traces of female hormones.

To prove their theory, they fed 100 men 12 pints of beer and observed that all of them started talking nonsense and couldn't drive.

Developed Entertainment District

Developed entertainment districts are high-density areas of operating and thriving bars, lounges and nightclubs. You will find a solid base of patrons already established.

Many of these concepts have been operating for years and others will come and go overnight. Many districts have extremely high rent costs and the landlords can gouge out the life of a successful bar with over-blown lease prices and ridiculous agreements with little or no TI dollars.

Let's look at what you can expect from an established entertainment district.

- High traffic;
- Established patronage;
- You will spend less on initial promotions;
- You can directly target advertisements to established patrons;
- Lots of other concepts are after the same patrons;
- Patrons spend less time in your concept and prefer to bar hop;
- You will most likely find and remodel an older concept;
- The area is zoned for bars already;
- Synergy is positive, not negative;
- Do not try to overlap concepts;
- Lots of established parking.

The developed entertainment district has lots of pros that outweigh the cons but you must remember you will be the new kid on the block and the other kids don't want an idiot messing things up.

The city will be closely monitoring districts such as this for DUIs, fights, underage drinking and deviant activities.

The local operators will already have reputations and working relationships with the authorities and you must work to make sure you don't rock the boat.

Lease Negotiation

This is the point where concepts succeed or fail. With one signature and a bad decision, you can doom your entire dream. Negotiating any lease is a pain in the butt, and if you feel you are getting a bad deal, you are!

Both parties in a lease negotiation are only trying to secure the best deal. If you feel your concept cannot succeed because of the high monthly cost of the lease driving deep into your profits, then you will need to rethink you location selection.

At this point, failure is not an option and the quickest way to sink your own ship before it even sets sail is to take on a huge monthly dept that will drag you into bankruptcy.

Thing to consider when negotiating for a new lease:
- The landlord is trying to make money;
- Research what other similar venues in the immediate area are paying for their leases;

Demographics

- Do not seem too eager;
- Get an attorney to review the final lease for you;
- Make sure the lease is affordable;
- Deal directly with the landlord if at all possible;
- Stay away from brokers with their fees;
- Ask for "TI" (tenant improvement) concessions;
- Make sure the venue has proper zoning;
- You will need to have enough time from when you sign the lease until you open because of construction. You do not want to pay the lease while you are under construction;
- You will need parking concessions for both the handicapped and patrons per city code.

Free Beer

Grazel and Dermot fancy a pint or two but don't have a lot of money.
All together they have a staggering 50 cents between them.
Grazel says, "Hang on, I have got an idea!" He went next door to the butcher and came out with one large sausage.
Dermot says, "Are you crazy? Now we haven't got any money left at all!"
Grazel says, "Don't worry, just follow me," and goes into the next pub where he immediately orders two pints and two large vodka and tonics.
Dermot says, "Now you have lost it! Do you know how much trouble we will be in? We haven't got any money!"
Grazel says, "Don't' worry, I have got a plan. Cheers!" So they have their drinks. Grazel says, "Okay, I will now stick the sausage through my zipper. You go on your knees and put it in your mouth." Said and done. The landlord notices it, goes berserk and throws them out. They continue this, pub after pub after pub after pub, getting more and more drunk—all for free.
At the 10th pub, Dermot says to Grazel, "I don't think I can continue this any longer. I am so drunk and my knees are killing me!"
Grazel says, "How do you think I feel? I lost the sausage in the third pub!

Bar Design

I have heard people comment how I am like Walt Disney. I didn't understand that for the longest time and finally had to ask. Here is the answer I received: "Walt Disney created a fantasy land for people to escape reality, even if only for a short while. Like going to never-never land" I have been creating small, fun adult Disneyland's.

"When designing, design for the animal!"

<u>Companionship</u>: **Like herds, flocks, gaggles, pods and packs of wild animals, we also group together to seek companionship, security and mates.**

<u>Comfort</u>: **Finding an example of comfort in the animal world can be as easy as going home each day and needing to kick your dog off of the couch. No matter how many times you yell at him, he just loves that spot!**

<u>Mating rituals</u>: **Mating in the animal world often consists of rituals and displays of dominance or availability. Such displays need an audience and are designed to attract or influence a potential mate in the selection process.**

You are designing your bar to promote social interactions for patrons who will want to experience a great time and feel comfortable in the environment. If you and your designer just throw in expensive décor, cool-looking objects and structures hoping to impress your patrons, then you do not understand the fickle nature of the beast. Patrons quickly become indifferent to your expensive décor if your venue has no soul or flow.

Designers often tend to design based on a budget. This means that they have one million dollars for design ideas. Designers will then look at the venue's layout and find six areas that will be the high-dollar design-item areas.

- Area 1 will get a budget of $100,000 to do a water effect;
- Area 2 will get a budget of $130,000 to do a mosaic glass effect;
- So on and so forth until the budget for the design items is exhausted.

When you walk through the building, you will have high-dollar, high-impact design hotspots to wow your guests with but no real comfort.

I have witnessed the most beautiful venues go out of business while shit-hole college bars make millions of dollars every year.

Why Is This and Why Does It Happen?

When choosing your designer or consultant choose carefully as an issue that I have run into many times is that designers don't design for people; they create temples and monoliths of selfish indulgence and transient worship to themselves.

Design can be whatever you imagine, and the limits are boundless. Enter a venue and envision the space filled to capacity with patrons. Imagine your staff under pulsing lights while music videos play on the plasma screens. Create a magical place.

The ideas that I put forth may work for some and not for others. These ideas are based on years of me literally living in bars and nightclubs. I have been creating and observing venues that do and do not function. I have learned through trial and error the critical mistakes made by industry professionals from every trade.

I have been witness to so many concepts designed by architects and designers who create products they do not understand. Yes, they can make it beautiful. And, yes, the owners can brag about spending millions of dollars to create Eden. But if Eden is boring, people will leave. Just ask Adam and Eve.

I would like to see a designer work behind a bar for one night or navigate tight pathways in high heels with a tray full of drinks.

I would love to watch an architect drag 5-gallon buckets of ice or trays of glassware from the basement to the bar on the second floor 20 times a night. How about having an interior designer cut a check every week out of his or her personal account to fix a rip in an exotic, $75-a-yard fabric that takes a week to order and another week to repair?

"Function and flow are key words in every concept!"

The Little Black Bar Book

My Money and Designing a Concept

Any design concept must minimize cost to maximize a speedy return of investment. This does not mean build a crappy product. This means do your research, get multiple bids and take time to investigate alternatives or cost-effective solutions to obtain the look and feel you desire.

Try to make $250,000 look like a million, if at all possible. Or at least don't waste your million. Below is a breakdown of different areas in the design process

Design

- Flow
- Concept ideas
- Entrance
- Bathrooms
- Seating
- Bar areas
- Kitchen
- Storage
- Energy points
- Décor
- Areas (VIP, dance floor, etc.)
- Audio
- Live music
- Video
- Lighting
- Attachment points
- Equipment and POS System

"Think Functionality"

Flow

Key factors are flow patterns for both your patrons and staff.

Flow patterns for your patrons are critical. This is the ability for patrons to walk around in search of potential mates or acquaintances. Creating eye contact and promoting social interaction is a huge factor in developing human relations. You must help to create connections between your patrons. Below are samples of flow patterns:

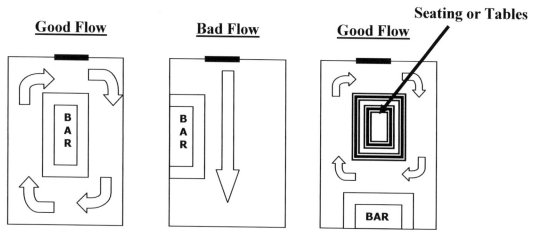

If a male patron in the <u>Bad Flow</u> example were to enter and see a girl he was interested in or wanted to get a better look at on the other side of the venue, he would have to walk straight back and then turn around, returning to the front in a straight line. As a man this can be very uncomfortable.

This is the runway effect, as it's like being a model who walks down a runway with everyone watching them.

"The Long Hall of Doom!"

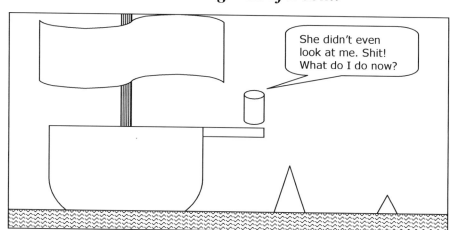

In the <u>Good Flow</u> design, the male patron can casually stroll around the venue and look as if he was just passing by.

Flow also will have an affect on your staff. Your staff's ability to move through the crowds quickly and effectively deliver drinks is critical to sales. Having pathways to and from the service wells for cocktail waitresses is essential.

Slow drink delivery times mean bad service and thirsty customers. From order placement to delivery should be less than five minutes, no matter what. For cocktail staff, that is a one-minute walk to the bar, one minute to order and get the bartender to make the drinks, and one minute to return to the customer. That leaves another two minutes to take more orders.

Concept Ideas

Keeping the concept and the design complementary is important. You need to create and design an ambiance and atmosphere for your venue to fit your concept.

Eclectic is a good description of many concept designs with compromises between principals, designers and budget restraints. The end product is often a mess.

When designing your concept, be creative and focus on everything. Even the smallest details are important. Below is an example of a check-list of ideas to bring to a beach-themed bar and grill to life.

"Stingray's Beach Bar and Grill"
1. Beach-style décor
2. Buckets of beer
3. Palm trees

4. Surfing posters
5. Surf boards
6. Tiki hut-style bar
7. Mexican food and seafood
8. Walls finished as wooden planks

Entrance

Designing an effective entryway for your concept is important. You don't want to give away too much to potential patrons. Mitigate exterior weather conditions and create a greeting platform.

The idea behind the barrier is to create or force a connection between the patron and the host or hostess. Immediate contact with a patron in the entrance can force a commitment from him or her. Once a greeting has been made, it is harder for patrons to walk away.

Once the patron has committed to entering the venue, he or she will encounter the barrier with a staff member offering a friendly greeting and offering to seat them immediately.

Hostess: "Welcome to Stingray's! Are you joining us for drinks or food tonight?"

Once contact is made, it is harder for a patron to tell the greeter, "No, thank you." The patron cannot see if the bar is slow or too busy and will make his or her decision based on the initial contact. You should not rely on other factors to capture that patron's business when a simple greeting can do it for you.

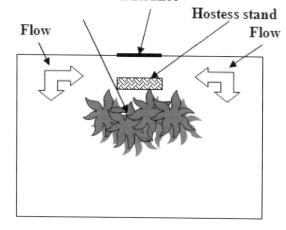

The Little Black Bar Book

Above, we are using the Stingray's concept and integration of concept and décor to create an effective barrier. The design works to create the initial impression of the concept. Using fake palm trees and a thatched hostess stand with a surfboard-style sign, we will set the tone of the concept with this first impression.

In creating your barrier, you can see how it works to inhibit the vision into the venue and also create a flow pattern upon entering. The style of barrier allows for you to keep the front doors wide open and allow the venue's music and energy to grab patrons' attention as they pass by.

This area allows for you to mitigate outside weather conditions such as cold, wind, rain and others.

This area also becomes a good platform for security to ID patrons as they enter.

Other good ideas to have at the entrance are:

1. Security camera with a recording system;
2. Photo ID scanner;
3. Breathalyzer;
4. POS system to take cover charges;
5. Upcoming-events advertisements;
6. A small audio speaker;
7. Menu display area.

Bathrooms

Designers, architects and owners all need to go to the busiest bar or nightclub in town during the peak hours of operation. Then go and stand in line to use the women's restroom. This is a line like the DMV. Once you get to the front, you find that trying to hover over a toilet in heels after three or four vodka Red Bulls, holding your skirt up and panties to the side, is a DUI test in itself.

In women's restrooms, no one wants to touch the toilet seats or flush the toilets, so heaps of paper clog the toilets and litter the floor. The women's restroom looks like a landfill by the end of the night.

This is a critical issue facing many bars and nightclubs. The lack of toilets for both women and men is a huge disservice to your patrons. Patrons are forced to stand in long lines while only trying to make more room for more beer and liquor!

Women are the worst victims of the low toilet count, and the lack of bathroom attendants compounds the situation. The women's toilet count should be double the men's and what the city planning department requires. City codes and requirements for the amount of toilets for women and men, including handicapped facilities, are based on occupancy levels.

For example, your occupancy is 100 but you can fit 300 patrons in your bar at one time, and have over 600 coming and going throughout the night. Based on these figures, there will not be enough toilets for the amount of patrons who pass through your venue if you only meet code requirements. You should, if at all possible, double the toilet count in the women's room.

Items Needed for Your Women's Room:

- Drink rails;
- Purse hooks in the stalls and at the sinks;
- Full-length mirrors;
- Trash cans with large mouths in every stall;
- Two or more trash cans in the common area;
- Bathroom attendant;
- Good, warm lighting with reds or pinks to give a healthy skin tone and make the girls feel and look good;
- Flush-valve toilets;
- Cleaning products storage area;
- Toilet ass gaskets
- Large-volume toilet-paper holders;
- Soft toilet paper (not sand paper).

The Little Black Bar Book

Items Needed for Your Men's Room:

- As many urinals as possible;
- Ash trays;
- Drink holders everywhere;
- Trash cans with large mouths in the common area;
- Tile on the walls up to 6 feet if possible;
- Stuff to read on the walls while guys piss: sports pages, jokes, girlie pictures, etc.;
- Urinal dividers ("Keep those wandering eyes off my private parts!");
- Standard sinks, nothing fancy, stainless steel if possible;
- Standard faucets, no long necks or fancy, long handles;
- Make everything simple to use and bulletproof (Tiled walls up to 6 ft and stone or ceramic tile on the floors along with granite countertops)

Seating

There are actually strategies for seating, and they are more complex than you would believe. Seating is both good and bad for business. Seating in any venue is an important decision, with many variables. You are able to choose from many styles of furniture to fit the needs of your venue.

The Internet can be a powerful tool in locating new and used furniture. You will be able to receive price estimates on a range of items if you think you're being overcharged by a local distributor.

Comfortable sitting will keep your patrons in your venue longer and make them happy! (Be aware that this can be both a Pro and Con at the same time.)

- Your patrons will spend more time seated, enjoying company and drinking and eating at a more relaxed pace. You will not be able to turn over high-quality seating that you might want set aside for high-dollar bottle sales throughout the evening.
- Patrons will use space needed for high turnovers throughout the night, potentially slowing the pace of your products being consumed.
- During slower periods, you will be able to entice and hold patrons in an empty venue easier and longer.
- The furniture is usually easier to damage.
- The furniture is often bulky and harder to move or remove from the venue.

Uncomfortable seating will keep your patrons rotating at a higher rate and allow you to focus on volume.

<u>Let's look at the pros and cons of standard seating.</u>
- In a high-volume venue, you can potentially turn patrons over more rapidly.
- The furniture is durable and will need little repair.
- The furniture is just uncomfortable—a real pain in the ass!
- The furniture is usually easy to store, move and stack.

<u>Let's look at the different types of seating available.</u>
1. Booths: These are comfortable and ideal for cozy, intimate gatherings. They are large and hard to move. A well-designed booth is sturdy, with good padding and a small recline to the back. The seat should be covered in a tough, easy-to-clean vinyl with a fabric or vinyl back.
   - A good booth will start at $100 per linear foot and be made from marine-grade plywood with foam and spring-seating support.

2. Bar stools: These staples of the industry come in many varieties and can be made from almost any material, including wood, metal, stone or plastic. Many cheap metal versions are available, though you should be wary as you will need to replace them often.
   - A good bar stool will be durable and sturdy, with a wide enough seat to fit most large-sized patrons.

3. Banquettes: These are expanded versions of a booth and can run any length. They are comfortable and add versatility to many venues. They can come in sections from 1 to 12 feet long, and can be used to create long banquette sectionals.
   - This style of seating is the same as a booth in its cost and design style.

4. Modular seating: This is a style of modern seating which commonly has no backrest and only a large, wide, cushioned seat. It can be easily moved and often has accompanying small square or circular pods. These can be arranged into numerous seating combinations.
   - Modular seating needs to be covered in vinyl as it will be spilled and stepped on

5. Couches and love seats: These are comfortable and can be covered in almost any fabric. The fabric can be easily removed and cheaply re-

covered off-site. They are ideal to create intimate seating areas with minimal cost.

6. **Tables:** The amount of tables and tabletop surfaces to choose from seems to be endless. Trying to keep the table or surfacing in line with the concept is easier now more than ever. Table styles can range from high-top and cocktail to booth and even larger custom communal tables. Even cheap coffee tables from a thrift store are common in bars and pubs. Here are a few different styles of tables to choose from, Coffee, Cocktail, Hightop and Communal tables

Choosing the right table for the right space, however, is tough as tables take up a lot of floor space and must be stable and durable as they will be moved often. Good tables also should take the weight of a person sitting on them.

7. **Drink rails-**The addition of drink rails throughout any venue will add functionality and can be used as a barrier for dance floors or VIP areas, in some cases. Drink rails can be stylish and decorative and will create great attachment points for your patrons to lean on or set their drink.

Seating as Attachment Points

Seating is an attachment point to which patrons are drawn. They become a home base of sorts to groups of patrons. Two different types of seating are communal seating and intimate seating. In communal seating, you have an area patrons can share. This area is great in creating social interaction between different groups and people. In intimate seating, you have more privacy, intimacy and security for those in your group and your belongings.

Creating Attachment Points

If you were to place six bar stools around a large high-top and allowed open seating, you would see it become an attachment point. Patrons need to be attached to something to feel comfortable. People don't feel comfortable standing out in an empty space. They like to lean against things such as a bar and have places to put their drinks.

Creating attachment points with furniture can be done easily and at anytime. Do not block traffic patterns. Creating attachment points can be cheap and easy to add and remove.

Bar Design

Who Can Say This Sentence?
The Taco Bell Chihuahua, a Doberman and a bulldog are in a bar having a drink when a great-looking female collie comes up to them and says, "Whoever can say liver and cheese in a sentence can have me."

So the Doberman says, "I love liver and cheese." The collie replies, "That's not good enough."

The bulldog says, "I hate liver and cheese." She says, "That's not creative enough."

Finally, the Chihuahua says, "Liver alone ... cheese mine."

Bar Areas

Choosing the type, placement and design of your bar is critical.

What is a Bar's Function?
A bar is a point of sale and storage for liquor, beer, wine or any other commodity you choose to sell or provide. The most important aspects of your bar design is functionality and efficiency.

The key to a well-designed bar is laying out your equipment so you can efficiently move high volumes of product during peak business hours. By providing the right tools and lay out to an experienced team, your customers should never have to wait more than 30 seconds for an acknowledgement and two minutes for service.

The Little Black Bar Book

Something to remember while designing your bar: *Every linear foot of your bar top is your own money-printing machine!*

Different types of bars and alcohol sales points available to you:

- Main bar;
- Satellite bar;
- Beer bar;
- Margarita bar;
- Sangria bar;
- Martini bar;
- Infusion bar;
- Beer tub or beer bath;
- Cocktail service well;
- Shot station with a roving shot girl.

Main Bar

Your main bar is the focal point, with multiple service wells and the majority of your cold storage and premium liquor storage.

<u>Cold beer</u>: Is there any other kind of beer to serve? You must design enough cold storage in your bar to handle a full night of service.

"The two types of wells are the service well for cocktails and the main wells for patrons."

<u>The Service Well:</u>
The service well should be situated at the end of the bar, with room for cocktail waitresses to work without interfering with prime bar frontage.

<u>Items for your service well:</u>
- Trash cans;
- Glassware;
- Table- or bottle-service items;
- Menu storage;
- POS terminal;
- Dry goods for service;
- Ice well with a soda gun.

The Main Well

Below is a standard layout that should be adopted for every bar! This is efficient for all right-handed bartenders.

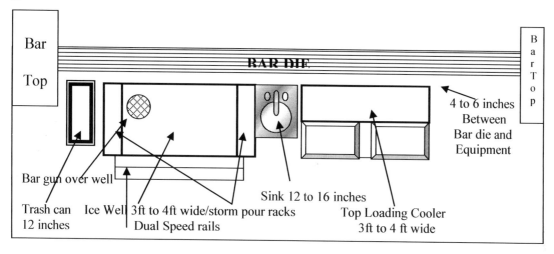

Steps in designing your back bar area:

- **The height of your bar should be 42 inches. The width of your bar top should be between 16 inches and 36 inches. The thickness of the bar top will be determined by the surface: granite, stone, marble, wood, glass, etc.**
- **The bar's floor should be a poured epoxy, water-proof concrete such as Duracrete/Quick Crete or Quarry tile flooring. All poured floors should have a non-slip shark's tooth grit added.**
- **All bars must be water-proof, and the inside of your bar die must be covered in FRP. Seal the inside with silicone so the back bar area can fill up with water and not leak in to ruin your expensive hardwood flooring.**
- **Your bar die should be made out of 2-foot by 6-foot framing, with marine-grade plywood on both sides. The front bar side can be covered in any décor you choose, but the inside must be covered in FRP because of health regulations.**
- **You will need to place a drain and run hot and cold water to all of the sinks at your bar. You will need a master shut-off valve behind the bar to meet health codes. Place the shut-off valve behind the trash location as the trash can be easily moved for access.**
- **You will need a power outlet near the ice well on a GFI circuit for a 12-inch to 18-inch florescent light mounted under the bar and over the ice well. You will also need power to run the compressor for your soda guns. One compressor can run two soda guns.**
- **Power is also required for your top-loading cooler. One 20-amp circuit will handle all three items: your light, compressor and top-loading cooler.**

The Little Black Bar Book

- You will need a raised floor drain under or near your sinks. You will also need a flush floor-drain, centered between your front and back bars, in a low spot for when you hose down and clean your bar every night.
- Your soda gun lines will run behind your bar equipment where you have left between 4 inches to 6 inches between your bar die and your bar equipment. It's a large and inflexible hose. The soda line will T off to each ice well, where it will be attached to the soda gun head and hose over each well. You will have a drain cup that will let draining liquid or spillage from the gun to run off into the raised drain under the sink.
- You will need space behind your equipment where you have left between 4 inches to 6 inches between your bar die and your equipment to make plumbing connections to your equipment.
- Dual speed rails should be attached to the front of your well for your main liquors. These provide easy access for the most commonly used liquors your bartenders will need. If space is an issue, you can also add a speed rail onto the front of your top-loading coolers.
- Spill trays will need to be placed flush in your bar top over the wells. This is to save your ice wells from spills that would run off the bar and into the ice well. The spill trays will need to run into the raised floor drain under your sink. These spill trays are between 4 inches and 6 inches wide but can be custom-made to any width or length. These should be close to the length of your ice well.

Satellite Bars

Satellite bars are important to 3,000 square-foot or larger venues. This size allows for an additional fully equipped and stocked bar for your patrons to access.

These satellite bars are often smaller than the main bar and positioned in areas to help boost sales and increase service time in busy venues.

A satellite bar, when correctly placed, cuts down on cocktail waitress travel time and increases the quality of service.

A VIP room can have its own satellite bar catering to those select patrons. This bar will hold more premium liquors and be better equipped for table and bottle service. It may have a cooler to keep liquor such as Champagne and premium vodka chilled for bottle service.

This bar is designed exactly the same as your main bar. (see above)

Beer Bar or Beer Garden

Beer bars or beer gardens work well servicing venues with high-volume beer sales. This includes draught, bottled and canned beer. Beer gardens are effective on large patios as you only will need electricity to run a cash register and the Kegerators for your draught beer.

As draught beer is a higher profit-margin product, many bars will offer multiple brands to their patrons by the glass, pint or pitcher.

Beer bottles and cans are faster to serve than cocktails, so you can move large amounts of beer in a short time.

Beer gardens can keep beer cold in many fashions, such as beer tubs or similar containers. Also, top-loading or back-bar coolers can be used.

Fact: Beer gets cold fastest in a mixture of ice and water!

Little or no plumbing is needed for beer gardens and these areas can be set up and completely removed in a short time. These areas can be temporary for special events or just the summer. Some bars can choose to create a more permanent version of this and utilize it year round.

Margarita or Daiquiri Bar

The addition of daiquiri or margarita machines can bring in huge profits.

Margarita bars are most often referred to as daiquiri bars. These are popular in warm-weather climates and provide a great high-profit addition to many concepts. Many chain bars have built and designed their entire concept around the sale of frozen daiquiris and margaritas.

The cost of installing an industrial-quality daiquiri bar can be high, with all the plumbing and electrical needs for each machine. The large-scale industrial machines need a constant flow of cold, running water to cool them and make high volumes of frozen beverages. Each industrial machine will need a 20-amp 208v or 220v power outlet on a GFI circuit.

The industrial versions can cost as much as $4,000 to $7,000 dollars each, but you can negotiate with the daiquiri mix supplier and you should be able to get the machines supplied to you at no cost. The supplier will own the machines and you will only have to buy the product and service the machines.

The cheaper plastic machines are great for low-volume margarita and daiquiri sales. These can be purchased for $1,000 to $3,000 each, and can have between one to three flavors in one machine. You can get a liquor company to donate these machines if you agree to only use their brand of liquor. These machines only need a 20-amp circuit for power and are easy to clean, operate and maintain.

Sangria Bar

This is a combination of fresh fruits and wine mixed to create a wonderful, fruity tasting concoction.

The equipment needed for this is a fresh-fruit chopping block, pitchers, a small push cart and chilled wine.

Martini Bar

Martini bars are a great addition to nightclubs or lounges. Imagine a free mix martini bar and its sour appletinis with flame-baked, caramelized sugar topping. It is a wonderful treat in any venue.

Watching a master mixologist create martini magic while dicing and slicing fresh fruits and combining infused liquors, premium liquors and fresh fruit mixers to create cocktail art is like having an acrobat in your venue. Patrons will be amazed while their cocktails are created in front of their eyes.

These bars can be very small in size with a simple sink, power for blenders or mixers, and a cash register.

Infusion Bar

Infusion bars are created with large glass vessels containing with fresh fruits or even Jolly Ranchers. These vessels are then filled with liquor, letting the contents marinate, and instilling the liquor with the additives' flavor.

For instance, adding watermelon Jolly Ranchers and letting them dissolve in vodka will give you a fantastically flavored watermelon vodka. The same is true for lemons, cinnamon, sour apples or any other fruit or flavor you want.

You only need a bartender who can do research and testing to create these wonderful and colorful infusions. The only items you will need are the glass vessels and the ingredients. The infusion vessels can be stored behind your main bar in a beautiful display for your patrons to see and experience.

Beer Tub or Beer Bath

This simple addition to any venue can easily move high volumes of cold bottled or canned beer to patrons.

Beer tubs or beer baths can be a temporary addition in any bar, and can be easily set up and removed every night. These metal or plastic vessels are designed to hold large amounts of ice and cold beer in cans or bottles. They are easy to refill and restock from cases of room-temperature beer stored nearby.

This is an extremely cheap revenue-generator. The beer bath or vessel will be given to you free from your beer distributor and comes in many different styles, shapes and colors.

There is no need for power or plumbing, as most beer baths are a cash-only point of sale. You must make sure that you have a good and accurate inventory and monitoring system for your beer bath, as this is an easy location for theft to occur by your employees.

The Little Black Bar Book

Cocktail Service Wells

Cocktail service wells are often placed on the ends of main or satellite bars, but can be located out of the way or hidden from public access with only cocktail waitresses and a service well bartender allowed in the area.

Separate cocktail service wells are small, fully functional and fully stocked. Service well bartenders can focus on service staff orders and fill orders faster than they would with patron interference.

The items needed are: trash cans, glassware, table- or bottle-service items, menu storage, POS terminal and dry goods. For the service well bar layout and design, see the Main Bar section above.

Shot Station and Roving Shot Girl

Shot stations are small service points for pre-made shots which can be made by your bartenders or purchased through distributors. You can order large varieties of shots in test tubes or Jell-O shots in an assortment of flavors.

You can have your roving shot girl's free-pour shots out of premixed bottles or carry trays of test tubes around the venue, hard-selling to customers.

Hiring shot girls to roam around wearing sexy outfits selling to patrons is a tough job. The prime candidates are girls with outgoing personalities, such as ex-high school cheerleaders.

The cost of a pre-made shot is pennies and the cost of pre-made test tube shots is less than 10 cents. You can see how the high profit-margin makes them well worth serving.

A good thing to remember is that a shot will not fill your customers' stomachs as a beer would so it will not conflict with him or her purchasing other beverages or food.

Kitchens

Designing and outfitting a good kitchen from scratch can cost hundreds of thousands of dollars. This is money well wasted on venues focused on selling and serving liquor and beer.

Many states and cities will require you to serve food! If you are forced to serve food in order to obtain licensing, you had better make it the best you can. If you are not a culinary wiz, then do some research to find out what the legal minimum requirements for food service are. Some license restrictions will require that a percentage of sales be derived from food sales. If necessary, you should find someone with experience and a passion to deliver high-quality food.

Needs of a kitchen are as follows:
- Grease trap;
- A hood system (cost about $1,000 per linear foot);
- Ansul Fire repellant system for the hood;
- FRP on all of the walls or ceramic tile;
- Drop ceilings need a double layer, with the bottom level being a vinyl wrap;
- Non-slip Quarry tile or epoxy floor;
- Floor drains;
- Three dunk sink;
- Hand sinks at every entrance;
- Proper lighting;
- Gas lines running to fryers and ovens;
- Mop closet;
- Chemical dish-washing system, often with a hood system;
- Dish tables and a rack system attached to your dishwasher;
- Refrigerators;
- Freezers;
- Hot or cold prep tables;
- Microwave oven;
- Convection ovens, stoves, fryers and grills.

Many of these items will depend on your menu. Once you begin to select your menu items, the proprietary items list will need to grow to fit the needs of that list.

Items such as plates, silverware, cookware, dry goods and so on will be added to the shopping list as the needs of your menu become clearer. As your menu expands, there is a greater need for refrigeration and you may need to invest in walk-in coolers and freezers.

If you are unsure what steps to take in developing a menu and kitchen, there are a number of experts who can help. You may need to hire a food and kitchen consultant to guide you through the issues of food service and I happen to know a few very talented consultants, Jeff Pappas or Nick Raymond.

Jeff Pappas is a distinguished and humble kitchen and restaurant guru who is more than capable of leading you through the pitfalls of the food world. He can create a menu designed around the restrictions you may face with a limited kitchen layout.

Jeff Pappas BMG Group 702-496-6582
Nick Raymond 702-203-6200

Storage

Besides bathrooms, this is one of the most overlooked areas of any venue. This is often a painful and uncomfortable blunder.

Designers and architects rarely have worked in a bar, nightclub or restaurant, and do not fully realize the huge amounts of space taken up by stock and dry goods. This will often leave the management team scrambling to design creative storage mechanisms, and may leave them fucked.

Types of items and the storage needed for them:
1. Liquor storage;
2. Premium liquor storage cages;
3. Beer storage in cases;
4. Dry goods storage for the bar;
5. Cold storage, such as a walk-in cooler.

Liquor storage
This type of storage is for your well liquors that will be delivered in the case loads. You should store these on shelves so they can easily be inventoried and accessed during your peak business hours.

Premium liquor storage cages
These should be metal cages for storing premium, high-dollar liquors. Using cages allows for easy viewing and inventory without having to unlock and open the doors. Your bar manager and GM will need keys, and during peak hours of operation, the bar-back should also have a key.

Bar Design

A sign-out sheet should be located inside or outside of the cage, and every bottle that leaves should be signed out with the brand, time and date.

Beer Storage

When you are short on space and getting ready for the weekend, you will have hundreds of cases of beer arriving daily. Where to unload and store it all can be a nightmare.

In the past, I have stacked beer high on the main floor of my bar and made it a décor piece. Patrons would take a few beers but never enough to matter, and the beer was warm so it tasted like donkey piss, anyway.

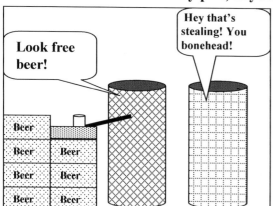 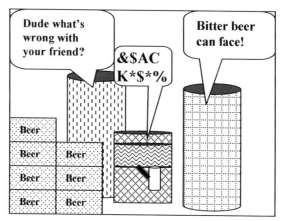

Keep the beer off the floor

Be careful that the floor does not become wet where you store your beer because the bottoms of the cardboard boxes will disintegrate. You will have a mess removing all the beer from the ruined cases.

Getting your beer into cold storage as quickly as possible is important to bring the beer to serving temperature. The ideal storage for cases of beer is large walk-in coolers where you can stack cases on elevated aluminum platforms.

The amount of storage room left aside for beer should be a full weekend's worth—with all the cold storage at your bars fully stocked.

Dry Goods Storage for the Bar

The amount of space needed for dry goods varies widely with the type of venue and concept.

A lounge, for example, will need plenty of glassware in many different styles. These will all need storage room. Dozens of cases of new glassware will need to be stocked to replace broken glassware. High-end lounges may also have to store tablecloths and napkins.

A bar that uses plastic stackable cups can maximize its use of space by stocking large quantities in boxes to the ceiling. Disposable cups are cheap, designed for single servings and then thrown away. Reusable plastic cups are also stackable and durable, allowing for less backup replacement stock.

Nightclubs can swing both ways with glassware: plastic or glass. Some nightclubs choose to use glassware for the VIP rooms and bottle service while using plastic disposable cups or reusable cups for the general public.

All bars and nightclubs will need to store huge amounts of items, and the most commonly used storage rack is called a "Metro rack." They are stainless steel racks that are easy to assemble and move. These shelves can be easily adjusted to fit the needs of the specific items you are storing.

Metro racks are strong, durable and lightweight. They also are approved for use by the health department.

Here are some commonly stored items: cherries, olives, napkins, mixes, cups, straws, cases of lemons and limes, buckets, cleaning products, ash trays and much more.

Cold Storage Such as Walk-In Coolers

Cold storage is important and costly. Buying and installing walk-in coolers can cost over $10,000 dollars. This is a steep price to pay for cold storage if it is not being utilized for a kitchen.

If a kitchen is involved, a walk-in is a must. Combination freezer/cooler units are the best buy and most efficient. In combination units, you first enter the cooler portion and then enter another door into the freezer portion.

Cold storage at the bar such as top-loading, deli-style and back-bar coolers are better options for a bar or nightclub. You can stock your beverages and then serve them directly to patrons. A bar or nightclub should have enough cold beverage storage for an entire weekend night's worth of beverages.

Energy Points

Patrons are looking for fun. You need to develop energy points to create an atmosphere and ambiance that entertains your customers. Energy points are items that hold the interest of your patrons in any form or function. This can be from a few seconds to hours.

Provide them with distractions from the grind. Take them away. Make them forget all of the stress, fatigue and drama of daily life.

Let's look at the different ways you can create energy in your venue using creative forms of distraction and entertainment.

Energy levels

High: These are items that are always changing and entertaining. They never do the same thing twice

Medium: These are items that change slowly or gradually over time. They have the ability to entertain and never grow old or boring.

Low: These items never change. They are interesting and might have a history or a story about them.

Below are items can be utilized to create an interesting environment.

You must be aware when placing items, how and where they are around the venue. For instance, placing too many high-energy items next to one another is not a good idea. You should spread them out so patrons gathered around a table can enjoy them.

High-Energy Points

- Bars: They have lots of activity and it is fun to watch beautiful staff and customers come and go. This social interaction zone is underrated for its entertainment value.
- TVs/video screens: These provide endless entertainment with a huge number of programming choices. I like to run music videos on half of the screens and cable programming on the other half.
- Go-go dancers: Make sure they're hot and can dance!
- Dance floor: Wide open, with a variety of lighting arrays

The Little Black Bar Book

- **People watching:** Of all of the energy points, this one has the most potential to amaze you.
- **Stage:** Many venues have staging that can be transformed for multiple uses, such as bands, VIP seating, stage shows, fashion shows and many other events
- **DJ booths-** DJ booths have become a focal point for patron and DJ interaction. DJs should be the entertainment coordinator for the venue. The DJ's job is to entertain customers by providing quality music, video and lighting programming.
- **Lighting effects:** This is critical in larger clubs with DJs where synchronizing the music with the lighting affects the entire venue's energy level. It sucks to hear a break-down in the music and see a huge lighting rig with all its lights zipping around the room flashing aimlessly. Hire a lighting guy who has a clue!
- **Stripper poles:** These are a low-energy point by themselves, but with a talented dancer, they can become true eye-candy!
- **Swings:** I love the ability to add fun-filled items for your team members. They can entertain everybody.
- **Mechanical bull:** Watching drunken people who can't walk straight try to ride a bull is entertainment! And what about bikini bull-riding?
- **LEDs:** These color-changing lights are a great addition. When used properly, they can be of great value, with entire color-changing walls, bars or even dance floors.
- **Patios:** These are more of an energy point directed at passing traffic. Just add a couple of TVs and bang!
- **Windows:** The view from some venues is worth the price you are paying for your lease.

These are a few of the high-energy points that can be used in your venue. Placement and use of these will vary with the layout, concept and design. Coming up with new ways to tantalize your patrons is a passion.

Medium-Level Energy Points

- **Fireplace:** This is always a great addition to any venue, and with the new ventless gas fireplaces, you can put one almost anywhere.
- **LEDs:** Yes, these again! But with good control and implementation, you can create a great ambience.
- **Aquarium:** These are beautiful but a pain in the ass! The fish die all the time, are poisoned by idiots who pour beer and liquor into the tanks. You should hire a full-time aquarium professional to manage these on a weekly basis.
- **Water features:** I love these, although they are a little played out. Recently, I have seen a new waterfall where the water "falls" upward in droplets. Even the addition of a standard waterfall adds energy to many venues.
- **Torches and other fire effects:** These are wonderful. When done by professionals who know how to handle fire effects, they can add a wow-factor to any venue.
- **Snow or bubble machines:** These are fun, versatile, cheap and easy to maintain.
- **Nitrogen systems:** These freezing blasts of cold are awesome. I never get tired of pushing the button and cooling down a hot, sweaty dance floor.
- **Electrostatic glass doors and walls:** These are cool and expensive, but I love the effect it has on bathroom doors when they are unlocked. The glass is clear, but once you lock the door, it becomes opaque.
- **Mirror balls:** Out of the past, cleaned up and spinning again, these are timeless. When utilized properly, you will get a great effect. Try having a mirror ball finished in all red mirrors. It's hot!

Low-Level Energy Points

- **Paintings:** You don't need to settle on a small portrait when you can take a photo and have it blown up 20 times its size. Then, create a huge frame from wood and frame the wall-sized portrait. Or you can just add a nail into the wall and hang what you've got.
- **Art:** Tastes in art are vastly different from one person to another so I can only say that looking at a bunch of dogs playing cards is still not cool.

- **Chandeliers:** These are hip and expensive and making a great comeback in the last few years with new styling and modern versions to fit any concept.
- **Metal, wood, stone sculptures:** Sculptures or giant stone balls floating in water and rotating are a couple of options. Great wood carvings and objects can bring the origins of your concept to your venue.
- **Stuffed animal heads:** I love a good moose head over a bar!
- **Décor pieces:** Décor pieces can come from finding objects that work with your concept. For an English-style pub, you can find old British items to place throughout your venue, such as flags, models of famous ships, ancient guns or old rum casks.
- **Paint effects:** Painting effects, such as sky motifs on the ceiling, are timeless, and if well done, look great. You also can make plain drywall look like aged wood, marble or maybe even aged plaster.
- **Plaster blocks:** These are amazing and come in hundreds of different designs. They can be stacked to create entire walls of intricate and amazing textures.
- **Textured walls:** Texturing walls with plaster or drywall mud can add wonderful, 3-D textures to a flat, plain wall. Just apply the mud or plaster in flowing patterns and sand the crap out of it. Then paint it white and add colored effect lighting. This is cheap, but messy and time-consuming to sand. This looks like a good time for a team-member pizza party!
- **Specialty glass:** You can use colored, cracked or even etched glass with your logo in the middle to create a nice conversation piece. The amount of different types of glass to choose from is vast. I have been using stained glass in my last few projects in a modern way, applying full sheets of one style to openings and windows.
- **Specialty metals:** Metals can bring a lot to a venue. I recently used a new stainless steel, stamped floor-tile to cover the entire front of a bar in Vegas. It was awesome! Can you see me patting myself on the back? Lots of new metals in sheet or tile form are on the market now. Magic Stone out of Los Angeles provided the tile for the Vegas job.

Energy points are important to not only you but your patrons, who will appreciate the thought that went into their great placement, whether they realize it or not. Often, one energy point will outshine all the rest and become part of the buzz surrounding your new venue. That buzz is what you will hear patrons tell their associates and peers: "Hey, you guys need to go down to that new bar/pub/nightclub and check out the coolest thing ever!" This is thanks enough for a job well done!

The overall success of your bar or nightclub will be measured by the experiences your patrons. Creating these experiences and bringing them to life on a daily and nightly basis is what I live for!

Décor

Décor and Your Concept

Choosing your concept often can be easier then choosing the décor. Once you have decided upon the concept, you want to take the next daunting step and choose the décor for thousands of square feet of ceiling, floors and walls.

I cannot tell you how to add décor to your venue as every one has so many different parameters. Concepts have different budgets, infrastructure, size constraints and timelines, along with endless other issues that make your venue different from every other one out there.

Choosing the décor that can create the ambiance you are looking for may be easy or extremely challenging. Often, you will spend long hours researching items to complete the feel and overall atmosphere.

Have you ever entered another venue and wondered how you can recreate that same feeling in yours? You might never be able to recreate that feeling because you are too close to your own concept. There is nothing magical about your venue, and you know who created it and how.

That magical feeling people find in some venues may be an accident or the result of true love and devotion to the concept. The magic even may be from the staff and not the venue.

Steps in Choosing Your Décor

Here is a relevant issue for 90 percent of projects that reach the construction phase: MONEY! CASH! CAPITAL! Yours or your investors', someone is putting up money to create your venue. The amount of money you invest in your concept is up to you. The idea is for you to get out and find creative ways to make your concept come alive for a price that is acceptable to you while still letting you achieve your overall vision.

The amount of money put toward your décor should be no more than 20 percent of your overall budget. Keeping that number low is up to you and how much you rely on your design group. Advise them that they need to think outside of the box!

Sometimes, big-ticket items will drive the cost of your décor budget upwards but is acceptable when you are certain that these items are vital to create your concept.

When picking décor items, you should stay within your concept guidelines. If you have an Irish pub, you won't need an LED color-changing bar. If you have a modern, high-end lounge, you won't want to put dead animal heads on the walls

Staying within the ideas for your venue and choosing appropriate décor items is not easy, but don't be afraid to look at what others have done and move in a similar direction. I am not saying to copy them, just follow their lead.

The Internet can be the salvation for many new projects, with prices for almost anything just a few clicks away. You can research décor items, purchase them and have them shipped to you in days. You can compare pricing construction materials such as floor tile or hardwood flooring from all over the world, and know that the price your contractor is giving you is fair.

You can view pictures of other concepts and share the images with your design team, who can then source the materials for you to match the look and feel you desire.

I feel that you or some member of your new team will have the creative ability to step up and put in some hard work and sweat for your concept.

Finding it inside yourself to pick up a paint brush, hammer or mop is fulfilling and will display your true desire in creating your concept to your team members.

"If you believe in your concept, then they must believe, also."

You do not need your contractor to decorate your venue, and you don't want to pay your contractor to do it. If you need a décor item that has special installation needs, let

your contractor install it. You do not need your contractor to help you paint walls, hang art or signage, or string Christmas lights.
Get off of your ass and delegate your team members to hang your moose head or paint the bathrooms. These are jobs that pizza party labor pays for!

You will need tools for your venue anyway, so go to the local hardware store and get a big tool box and fill it up with all of the equipment you can: screwdrivers, screws, hammers, nails, saws, screw guns, paint brushes, rollers and lots of cleaning supplies. You will need these items, and many more, to perform daily repairs to your busy venue.

You need to advise your contractor that when a new wall is finished, you will be painting it with your own outside painters or in-house team. Finding cheap labor to perform construction-style projects after you have your C of O or TCO will save you lots of cash. Some contractors will let outside trades in to work on décor style projects while the contractor is doing construction.

Contractors do not like this, and you should have an understanding with your contractor that you will be performing in-house décor projects while construction is still going on and before finals."

Some items must be completed for the city and you must allow your contractor to complete this work before you begin your décor process.

Projects such as running your sound and video-system cables need to be done in tandem with your construction, and these outside installers will need to run their wiring during construction. You do not want the electricians to run and supply these cables as the price will be outrageous.

Areas

Creating different types of areas throughout your venue is a bonus to your patrons, who will have added options to choose from as their mood changes or as your customer selection policies dictate. You can integrate multiple areas into one venue, designed to enhance your patrons' overall experience in the concept.

Your responsibility as an operator of a social gathering place is to facilitate to the best of your ability a positive social interaction environment for your patrons!

Bar Psychology

If you enter a 6,500 square-foot venue and there are 200 patrons, the venue looks practically empty! You and your friends will look at each other and say, "This place is dead and it sucks. Let's go!"

If you take the exact same 200 patrons but them into a 2,500 square-foot venue, you and your friends will walk in and think the place is off the hook!

Space management for your concept is important, and the ability to create different areas and manage their opening and closing to the public during business hours is critical to your guests' overall experience.

Different types of areas:
1. VIP room
2. VIP seating area
3. Raised seating
4. Dining area
5. Dance floor
6. Patio
7. Communal area
8. Attached lounge

VIP room

A great VIP room allows for a completely separate environment from the common public area, with limited access points such as doors, elevators, velvet ropes or a complete second level.

VIP rooms should be positioned so VIPs can have an elevated perspective of the common area. Separating your VIP room and common area with large glass walls is a preferred scenario.

VIPs should be able to enjoy a separate style of music at lower volumes, letting them interact without yelling to one another.

VIP room access should be regulated with special identifying badges such as a stamp or wristband, allowing your security to separate and identify the regular customer from the VIP quickly.

VIP rooms need to offer comfortable and intimate seating along with exceptional service from cocktail and bar staff.

This area enjoys the most success when it is raised one or two steps above the common area.

Think of this area like a king's throne, where the king is always elevated and seated above the commoners.

Raised seating

This is raised seating for the regular patrons. Raising seating areas in common areas creates a break in elevation in a large, flat, open area. Raising an area even one step and adding a drink rail around this area adds a cozy, little area where traffic patterns are not going to disturb the seated patrons.

You easily can segregate this area with some temporary partitions or concept-matching décor items, making it more intimate. Items such as plants such as bamboo or palms; cloth, beaded or metal curtains; glass; etc. The choices are limitless. With a little creativity, you will have created an entirely new area in your venue.

The seating options can be varied, with restaurant-style seating if you need to serve food, or a more casual seating with couches and love seats. You will be able to make your decision based on the size of the area and the different seating types that fit into your concept.

Dining Areas

If your venue needs to serve food, you will need dining areas to handle this as not everyone wants to sit at the bar and eat.

You must provide adequate seating for your patrons who are dining, and make that same seating versatile for your late-night guests. Finding a happy medium for both without having to move furniture in and out of the space everyday is important.

Begin by placing your seating selections out of traffic patterns and along walls. This will least affect the busy late-night hours' flow patterns. Make sure the furniture and tables you select are sturdy and firm, as late-night patrons will be far harsher on those items.

If you have created any of the raised sections described earlier, these will make great, versatile dining areas.

In your initial design phase, you need to assess the required space you feel will be needed for dining tables and seating, then integrate this into your bar or nightclub concept. Designing and outfitting your concept for a successful food-service business requires planning from experienced food-service professionals.

Dance Floors

This focal point of social interaction is a staple of every nightclub in the world. Some dance floors are too big, some too small, and some clubs have two or even three dance floors on different levels.

In selecting a dance floor location, you should place it with traffic patterns rotating around it. Putting a dance floor in the corner is not recommended as it will create two traffic stops and kill your venue's flow.

Raising your dance floor is okay, but I prefer to lower it by raising the surrounding floor, if you have the available ceiling height. This will let patrons look down over a crowded dance floor, elevating your people watching factor while increasing the effectiveness of this energy point. The lowered dance floor also will help create social interaction opportunities by helping customers locate other guests.

Providing small raised platforms for women to dance on are a great addition to any dance floor. Raised platforms let female patrons dance unmolested from frisky male customers. These platforms will need to have some sort of railing system so that intoxicated women don't accidentally fall off.

Raised go-go platforms with hired dancers are common and serve to offer eye-candy to male patrons. Go-go dancers also help entice customers to get out on the dance floor and dance.

Well-designed dance floors are made using a wooden floating floor system. Wood is a softer surface and allows for flex and absorption so that patrons' knees and feet are not sore after a long night of dancing.

Deciding on your dance floors the size will depend on the size of your venue and your type of concept. If you create a dance floor too large, you can always add seating, such as couches or booths, at the edges to take up the extra space by creating a VIP seating area. Having a dance floor too small can be like watching 50 clowns pile into a small car.

Shorting your venue on dance-floor size will be harder to correct. But the main consideration to take into account in designing your dance floor is the allowance of unhindered traffic patterns. You will need to allocate space for your pathways around the dance floor first and foremost! Your flow is the most important factor, and foreseeing and preventing traffic jams in bars and nightclubs is never an easy task!

So remember
"Flow, then Floor!"

Patios

I love good patios, and if you were to ask me if your venue needs a patio, I would immediately answer, "Hell, yeah!" Patios are awesome and provide an escape from the madness inside a bar or nightclub. Patios also allow for fresh air and a quieter location to be social.

Great patios offer some form of seating, and you should provide weatherproof seating that is durable, simple to stack and easy to remove. I recommend designing it with a large, glass, garage-door system that can open up to the entire venue, letting the inside ambiance wash out onto the patio and beyond, attracting more patrons from off the street.

Patio size is always an issue, and even the addition of bistro-style, street-side seating is great if that is all you are allowed.

Patios are not just for spring and summer. You can now use patios all year thanks to overhangs or by encasing the entire space.

When designing your patio, you may want to add a fire pit or communal fireplace for cold nights, or even a waterfall to cool down customers during the hot summer.

Because of liquor licensing, your patio should have a barrier from the public walkway and you should not allow unsupervised access to your venue. Barriers between the patio and public areas can be created using a short pony wall, metal railings or even planters. This is important in preventing underage people or unwanted patrons into your venue.

Make sure that if your lease lets you add a patio, that you would not be adding square footage onto your rent payments. This never should be an added cost to a lease, as you can argue that the space is only usable for a short period throughout the year and is not part of the building's permanent structure.

Communal Area

Communal areas are where most of your patrons will mingle and gather. Keeping this area comfortable with seating, attachment points and pathways are all important to keep the masses happy.

Let us not forget that every patron, from the super VIP to the regular Joe Schmo, need to share in the same high-quality fundamentals of service, seating and experience that you would expect to get yourself in any venue. It is your responsibility to provide a comfortable and safe environment designed to create social interaction opportunities for them.

Communal areas need to be designed to help increase mingling opportunities by forcing patrons into situations were communication and interaction are inevitable.

The Little Black Bar Book

How do you create a communal area? Here are some ideas:
1. Provide open seating gathered around one large table for patrons to share;
2. Position couches or love seats in patterns that force customers to look across and make eye contact with each other;
3. Position drink rails throughout the venue where people can randomly attach themselves next to other patrons;
4. Add modern modular seating without backs so they can be shared by patrons and easily moved around the room. The modular seating should originally be arranged with a communal setting in mind;
5. Add open seating around a fireplace;
6. Provide bar stools at the bar;

"Your must remember that your patrons do not come to your bar to get drunk, they come to socialize"

Attached Lounge
Many larger venues have the ability to add a separate lounge with a fully stocked bar which can be a completely different concept or environment, enhancing your patrons' experience.

Attached lounges are fun and you can add creative additions and social interaction activities such as pool tables, video games or ping pong tables. You can be creative and have tournaments and nightly competitions, with gifts, giveaways and prizes.

The attached lounge will add another point-of-sale to your venue. You could possibly add $5,000 to $8,000 in weekly sales. You also benefit by creatively utilizing your space.

Another benefit of an attached lounge is that it does not always have to be open, letting you control your overall space usage. If you are open on a weekday and your venue is slow, you will want to close down your additional lounge area. On the weekends, you will need to provide the extra space for your patrons.

Audio System

A good audio system does not have to cost an arm and a leg, and the possibility of getting the shaft when you are purchasing an audio system is huge. Bar and nightclub owners and principals are often at the mercy of A/V companies and don't understand what is needed for their venue and how much it truly will cost them.

Your audio system's placement and design is important, and a poor layout can have a negative effect on service provided by your team members. A bad sound system also can create a negative experience for your patrons.

One of the biggest mistakes with installing sound systems in bars and nightclubs is putting huge speakers in the room's four corners, facing into the center. This might work in a small venue, or even positioned over a small dance floor, but it is not the correct layout for the majority of sound systems.

Putting speakers in the corners will create hot zones which will be comfortable for patrons in the middle of the dance floor but blast those who are close to the speakers.

In the case of a larger dance floor, you should spread your sound system over the dance floor to reduce the hot spots. Place your speakers in the ceiling, equal distances from one another, to give you even coverage of the entire dance floor.

You will use a larger number of smaller speakers, but you will not need to drive them hard because of the even coverage and because your customers' bodies won't absorb the sound as it travels across the dance floor as it would in the four corners configuration. Smaller speakers also will cost less but you will need additional amplifiers.

It is important that the DJ has a good view of the dance floor from his booth. A good DJ must be able to read the patrons' reactions to the music and be able to react to what is working and how certain types of music are affecting the crowd. Your booth needs to be large enough for all of your equipment, the DJ, the DJs albums if he is spinning vinyl, and if need be, the lighting guy and his equipment and the video system, and still have space for them to work comfortably for long hours. Your DJ booth should be no smaller than 15 feet by 15 feet.

You will need to place your sound-system controllers and amplifiers in a secure, easily accessible location, with proper cooling and power. This is important because constant monitoring, cleaning and servicing are required. If at all possible, the booth is the perfect location for all of the components.

Your sound system will require ample clean power for the amplifiers and cable runs to the speakers. Some cities and states require that all low-voltage cables must be run in conduit to the speakers from the amplifiers. You will need to have this and the required power outlets for the amplifiers and DJ system in the DJ booth on your blueprints for the city planning department for approval.

Also, I recommend you use a ground loop isolator. This will keep feedback from other electronic devices in the building from getting into your sound system and creating a hum! The ground loop isolator should provide the power for all of your amplifiers, processors and DJ booth sound equipment.

Some of the major suppliers of audio systems for nightclubs and bars:
1. Mach Audio
2. JBL
3. Turbo Sound
4. Martin UK
5. EV
6. Crest Audio
7. Crown Audio
8. Function One

Bar Design

Let's look at placement of speakers and bar locations:

Below you can see how placing the speaker over the bar aimed into the venue lowers the volume of the sound for the bartender as the sound passes over the bartender.

Below you can see how placing the speaker behind the bar aimed into the venue places the bartender and the patron directly into the sound waves from the speaker

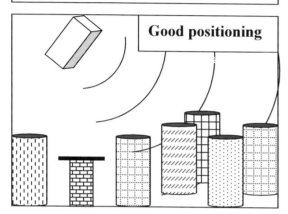

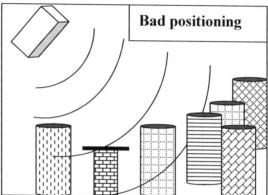

The Story of a Very Short Man

A man walks into a bar and says, "Bartender, give me two shots." The bartender asks, "You want them both now or one at a time?" The guy says," Oh, I want them both now. One's for me and one's for this little guy here," and he pulls a tiny, 3-inch man out of his pocket.

The bartender asks "He can drink?"

"Oh, sure. He can drink."

So the bartender pours the shots, and sure enough, the little guy drinks it all up.

"That's amazing" says the bartender. "What else can he do? Can he walk?"
The man flicks a quarter down to the end of the bar and says, "Hey, Jake. Go get that." The little guy runs down to the end of the bar and picks up the quarter. Then he runs back down and gives it to the man.

The bartender is in total shock. "That's amazing" he says, "What else can he do? Does he talk?" The man says, "Sure, he talks. Hey, Jake, tell him about that time we were in Africa and you made fun of that witch doctor's powers!"

The Little Black Bar Book

Below you can see the different volume zones These can be measured in decibels or db The db should decrease as they get closer to your bartender If the over all volume of your bar is 110db the volume for the bartender needs to be lower so that your bartenders can hear the orders from the patrons.

Below you can see how the sound waves are directly hitting the bartender and patron and the volume zones for both are too high.
The bartender will have difficulty hearing orders from the patron

90 db	100db	110db
-20 db	-10 db	+/-0 db
Medium	Loud	Louder

Bartender ↓   Patron ↓

100 db	110 db	+110 db
-10 db	+/-0 db	+10 db
Loud	Louder	Loudest

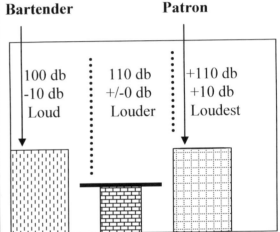

Below the patron calls out the drink order to the Bartender who is in a quieter zone so can hear the order easily from the patron

Below the bartender will still have to speak up for the patron to hear the amount of money needed for the transaction.

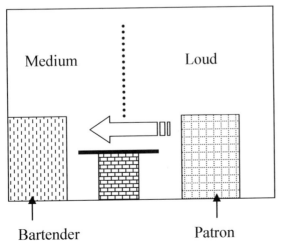

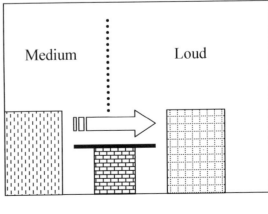

Bar Design

Let's look at speaker coverage in a bar or nightclub:

As stated above, a good, even coverage in a bar or nightclub, with as few hot zones as possible, works best. You will not have to increase the overall volume and you can have the same volume evenly covering your entire venue. With more speakers, you will be able to better control the volumes in your different areas, letting your patrons hold conversations without yelling into each others' ears.

Below you can see how we will use smaller Speakers to cover the venue evenly with sound eliminating hot zones. The small speakers on the perimeter of the venue are facing straight down providing even coverage for seating and walkways. The perimeter speaker's volume should be lower than the dance floor volume allowing your Patrons to interact without yelling.

Below you can see the typical four corner installation with four hot zones and uneven coverage of the venue These speakers need to be larger to project the sound to the dance floor and to be able to handle being over driven in order to achieve the desired volume on the dance floor. This is the most common mistake of many installers who find this easier to wire and install.

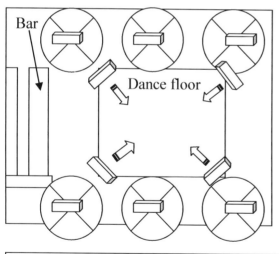

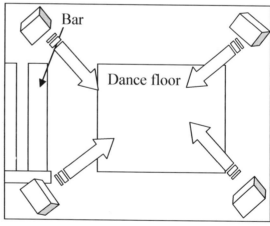

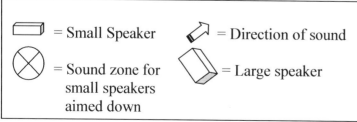

Some Questions You May Need to Know About Your Sound System

How much should I pay?
In a nightclub, you will need to dedicate more of your budget to your sound and lighting systems. You can expect to spend up to 20 percent of your entire budget on your lighting, sound and video systems with the installation, power and conduits.

What type of speakers will I need?
There are three types of speakers for you to purchase:
1. Subwoofers: These will provide the booming bass for your sound system and come in 15-inch to 18-inch sizes. Larger versions also are available. Subwoofers come in different styles and configurations for different applications. You can have short-, medium- and long-throw subwoofer enclosures and speakers. Depending on your placement and your venue, you may need one or more styles.
    The boxes or cabinets that the subwoofers come in make a difference in both sound and distance applications. You have the front-loaded subwoofers, in which you can see one or more subwoofers on the face of the box or cabinet. These are for medium- or long-throw applications. You also have a band-pass style box or cabinet that has the speaker buried inside of the box and cannot be seen. This is for shorter-throw applications.
2. Cluster horn or tweeter systems: These are small clusters of horns positioned over a dance floor, giving 360-degree coverage of clear, crisp high frequencies.
3. Top boxes: These are the mid-, full- or high-range cabinets for vocals. These come in many different styles and sizes, from 6-inch to 15-inch speakers or drivers, and may have more than one size speaker or driver. These also will have 1- or 2-inch horns or tweeters for the high ranges.
    - Many of these boxes can be configured using crossovers that are provided internally, or the crossovers can be configured into two- or three-way amplification, allowing your amplifiers and processors to directly feed the source signal to each speaker.

Top boxes are dynamic and come in many versatile styles and sizes. They can be nicely hidden in ceilings, tucked into ceiling soffit's hidden out of view, or displayed proudly with your lighting system.

In smaller venues, I like to use 8-inch top boxes running full range over the seating and communal areas, and 12-inch top boxes running two-way over the dance floor area. For the subwoofers, I would use multiple dual 18-inch subwoofer boxes.

In larger club venues, I prefer 8-inch top boxes running full range in the VIP room, 10-inch top boxes running full range in the common or seating area, and 15-inch top boxes running two-way over the dance floor. The subwoofers would be dual 18-inch to shake the building to the ground.

What type of amplifiers will I need?

I would recommend using the new digital amplifiers, as they are able to handle lower OHM loads and do not create as much heat as conventional amplifiers. But these are more expensive and you can often get two conventional amplifiers for the price of one digital.

What type of controller do I need?

You will only need one digital processor to control your standard size system in a larger venue. With multiple areas playing the same or different source music, you may need more processors.

What is a system controller?

These are great but dangerous, as they control your entire system from remote key pad locations or even wireless controls. In the hands of managers and team members, these become evil tools of doom! Beware! It may be cheaper and easier to arrange for your manager to just disappear (wink, wink) than to get your sound system fixed!

These are great tools, just keep them in the hands of a team member who has been trained in how to operate and control the system.

What type of equipment do I need for my DJ booth?
- (2) Pro DJ turntable CD players;
- (2) Turntable DVD players;
- (1) Four-channel DJ mixer;
- (2) Professional grade turntables;
- (1) Final scratch system;
- (1) DJ monitor or speaker, preferably self-powered;
- (3) Separate power circuits from your isolation transformer;
- (3) Surge-protector power strips;
- A location for the DJ to place his music collection;
- An ashtray and drink holder! These assholes will get drunk and spill every where;
- An extra seat for the DJ's ego to sit in!

"DJ DRAMA"

What should I pay an in-house DJ?
In a smaller venue, I would pay no more than $200 dollars a night, and guarantee him two to three nights per week. In a larger nightclub, you can expect to pay a talented Local DJ with a name and following up to $500 dollars each night, if not more. Paying international talent, on the other hand, can run you from thousands to tens of thousands of dollars for a quick two-hour set.

Who should maintain my sound system?
If you do not have an in-house lighting guy who will clean and maintain your sound system, you need a service agreement with the original installer.

New video DJ/VJ computer systems
This is kryptonite to DJs! They will hate you and the representative immediately. These new systems are incredible, and I have installed one in every venue I have done over the last few years.

The new Screenplay system by Nightlife has over 8,200 music videos stored on one computer system, and can play music prearranged in categories targeting your demographics. The Screenplay system also lets you create your own playlist from thousands of songs and then mix them together exactly how you like, including based on beats per minute

The system costs around $8,000 but can be leased. The music update CDs come every month to keep you current with the newest videos.

This system can run 24 hours a day, seven days a week without repeating itself, and will always keep the entertainment level going. The cost of this system vs. the cost of a DJ will have the DJ losing hands down every time. *Soon, large hard drives will replace the large egos of DJs.*

Is this system for my venue?
This system is designed to accommodate every venue. The only case for this not fitting is the mega-club setting, where the music needs to flow nonstop from beat to beat. Even then, it is a good system to have in place for early hours or off nights.

Is the system easy to use?
This is so easy that I put it behind my main bar and let the team members operate it all night.

Here are some of the things you will need for the Screenplay system:
1. (1) Screenplay system from Nightlife;
2. (1) 17- to 19-inch flat-panel monitor (included);
3. (1) video switching unit;
4. Clean power from your isolation transformer;
5. Patch cables to connect to your mixing console and video screens or TVs.

Screenplay Contact info: Kevin Frazoni 206-349-8784
Lighting

Different types of lighting are available. The first is conventional or architectural lighting, such as track lighting, florescent lighting, neon, chandeliers, and pendants or recessed lighting cans in the ceiling. All of these will contribute to your venue's overall ambiance, and some will be needed for general or cleaning lighting.

You can never have enough lighting, and creating the mood in your concept is one of those critical items that you must not fail! More is better! I say this because you can always turn the lights off or down with dimmers, and adding lighting at a later date is more expensive than just turning off lights or replacing bad lighting with fixtures that work for that area.

Nothing is more powerful in creating the mood you are looking for than the lighting of that area! If you choose the wrong color or are too dark or too bright, you will fail to capture the feeling you are trying to achieve.

Track lighting
Track lighting is one of the most versatile of all conventional lighting systems, with the ability to expand in almost any direction with relative ease. There is an endless selection

of different types and styles of lighting fixtures that can be attached to the track system, which makes finding the right light for the right job easy. Many new, beautiful glass or ceramic pendant fixtures are now available and are very cost-effective.

Florescent

Florescent lighting is always needed under your bar top to illuminate your ice bins and storage, kitchen and office areas. Florescent lighting can be used in the bathrooms in conjunction with recessed cans, creating a well-lit toilet area.

One of the biggest drawbacks of florescent lighting is that it cannot be dimmed well and exact light levels are harder to set.

The biggest advantage to a florescent fixture is its long life and dependability.

Neon

Neon is a bad word to many designers, but the truth is that neon is the overachiever! Of all conventional lights available, neon is often looked at as an eyesore by many designers. This is a light that will never burn out. One negative about neon is that it is fragile and harder to removed and reuse for other applications, such as for a remodel.

Neon is used mainly in signage, but also has many uses inside your venue, such as in lighting soffits in the ceiling or back-lighting glass displays. Neon beer signs are popular and are a powerful advertisement tool in a bar.

Using neon tubes in the ceiling and connecting them to your lighting controller can create an exciting lighting effect for your nightclub.

-What is neon? Neon is a glass tube filled with different types of gas. The different frequencies of the transformers create the different colors, with two electrodes on either end of the neon tube. Once electricity runs into the glass tube from one end, it excites the gases inside and creates a glowing effect.

-How much does neon cost? Neon is very inexpensive and is often priced by the foot, so it is easy to formulate how much you will need when getting a bid from a supplier. Don't forget you will need transformers, attachment clips and installation added in the bid.

-Can neon change color? Yes but it is more expensive than LEDs and not cost-effective.

-Is neon dimmable? Yes, it is, and you will need to let your sales rep and installer know you need special dimmable transformers.

Chandeliers
Chandeliers are making a big comeback and the endless types of new styles can fit almost any concept. They are never cheap but are very classy. Adding different color lights or LEDs will make them a very hip and dynamic addition to your VIP room or entryway.

Pendants
This fixture, which hangs from the ceiling or off of a wall, is a great way to add depth to a room while keeping hold of the venue's design parameters. Pendants hanging over VIP tables, dining tables, bar tops or down the center of hallways adds depth and creates little energy points in any venue.

Pendants most often come in glass or ceramic, but you can find them in metal, treated wood or even plastic. They can range from holy-shit expensive to damn-that's-cheap! If your pendants are not on a track light system, then you will need exact locations in you ceiling for a J-box or a 4s box for your electrician to mount these to, along with a dimmer to control the light levels.

Pendants often have matching wall sconces that keep the light source in one room consistent with the look and style. These are great to illuminate columns or highlight wall coverings or exotic or elaborate wall finishes, such as an elaborate wall paper.

Recessed ceiling cans
These are lighting vessels in the shape of a can, with a rounded top. They are installed so they are tucked up into the ceiling. Once you add a light bulb, they will project light onto the area directly below them.

These also come in a dynamic range of different styles and designs. The cost can range from $100 each to $250 each or more, and you will need to specify the light bulb you want, such as a spot or a wash, and the wattage.

Table or floor lamps
How can I forget the standard lamp? It is inexpensive and so versatile that you can get them anywhere and they can sit on any table or stand! The taller stand-up styles can sit on the floor.

These are cheap and easy to experiment with, and if they don't work, you can give them to your employees as gifts.

Intelligent lighting

Another type of lighting is intelligent or effect lighting, such as moving head lights or mirrored moving fixtures. These are operated from a lighting controller. Other effect lights that do not move but create moving, color-changing patterns also are available. One of the most popular effect lights used in every nightclub is the common strobe light. These moving and non-moving effect lights are what you find over a dance floor in nightclubs all over the world, and are the key to integrating the music and the sound into one entity.

Major intelligent lighting and effect lighting manufacturers:
1. Martin Lighting
2. Highend
3. Coemar
4. American DJ
5. Clay Paky

Mirrored and moving head lights

All of the high-end intelligent lighting manufacturers have high-quality, intelligent, moving light fixtures. These dynamic lights can be operated via a DMX lighting controller, that when programmed, can run detailed and precise patterns while changing colors, Strobing, changing gobo's or patterns, zooming, focusing and much more.

These lights are a must-have for any nightclub, and a good lighting operator can make the lights and music work together as one.

Do I need a lighting guy?

If you are a nightclub, yes! If you are a bar, no! If you have bands or specialty acts, yes, but on an event-only basis. Nightclub lighting rigs are normally much larger and far more complex than a bar's lighting rig, and are needed as part of the overall experience for the patrons.

If you are a nightclub and have a $100,000 lighting rig, please pay for a lighting guy!

What should I pay a lighting guy?

Depending on his experience and expertise in cleaning, repairing the lighting fixtures and programming and operating the lighting controller, you can expect to pay between $100 to $300 per night.

Bar Design

How many intelligent lights do I need?
I have seen many instances of nightclubs and bars that have been oversold equipment that is just not right or is overkill for the venue. Here is what you need to do: Contact three or more A/V companies and have them give you a proposal, along with a potential design layout for your venue. Then compare all three quotes and layouts. If at all possible, go and look and listen to other sound systems they have done. Ask the principal of those venues what he or she thinks about the quality of equipment, service and installation provided by the A/V company.

A standard nightclub should never need more than 12 moving lights with 24 effect lights as filler. The effect lights can be a mixture of strobes, par cans and DMX controllable effect lights.

How much service will my lighting rig need?
With proper monthly cleaning, you will need little maintenance and only need to change the light bulbs.

What types of moving lights are there?
You have two styles of moving lights. One is a moving mirror fixture and the other is a moving head fixture.

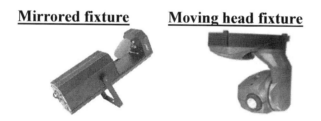

Mirrored fixture   Moving head fixture

What is the difference?
Moving mirror fixtures are faster and better for a nightclub with a high-energy music format. Moving head fixtures are slower, have more moving parts and will need more maintenance.

Which type should I get?
I would not split the lighting rig into two types of moving fixture as this will give you an inconsistent look. In the case of a venue with a low ceiling, you will want to use mirrored fixtures. The Techno Beam by Highend Systems is a good example of a wide-angle mirrored fixture for low-ceiling applications. If your venue plays electronic music, I would use mirrored fixtures. In a venue that has a stage, I would use moving head

fixtures. For all other venues, I would use moving head fixtures, as they add a show of their own when they are dancing around the ceiling.

What shouldn't I buy?
Never buy a moving head light wash fixture unless you are a concert hall. You are getting ripped off! Buy a regular moving head fixture that has gobos, and you can take it all the way out of focus with an open gobo and a prism effect and get a similar wash effect!

What do I need to hang my lights?
You will need some way to attach your lights, and the most common way is with an aluminum lighting truss system. You can attach the lights with clamps onto any pipe or steel bar that can bear the weight. Make sure your truss or piping is hung by a professional rigger. I would recommend using a local licensed and bonded rigging company.

What do I need for power?
For every three moving lights you hang, you will need one 20-amp outlet. You should not have more than three lights on one circuit. Your A/V company will need to tell your electrician where to locate the power and the power requirements for the fixtures. The lighting and the power locations and requirements should be shown on the blueprints that go to the city before construction. You may be required by the city to run your control cable in a conduit from your lighting controller to your lighting truss.

Don't I need a fog machine?
Yes, this is what will bring your light show to life, as the fog and haze catch the beams of color as they pass through the air.

What is the difference between a fogger and a hazer?
A fogger creates bursts of a dense fog that dissipates over a short period of time, often depending on your HVAC system. A hazer creates a fine mist that blankets the entire room with even coverage.

Both Hazers and foggers need to have a special mixture of fluid added to the machine to let them create the effects. The cost of the fluid is between $12 and $24 per gallon, and you can purchase it by the case or by the pallet and get a discounted price.

Foggers and Hazers can be controlled remotely with supplied equipment. The more expensive versions will work with your lighting control console, using a DMX control.

You will need to move your fogger or hazer around to find the right location in your venue as the HVAC or air currents will sweep the effect away from your dance floor and light show.

Non-moving, color-changing effects

You have the option of installing non-moving, color-changing lights, such as color-changing washes, fiber optics or LEDs.

These can be operated by internally supplied controllers, such as a DMX lighting controller or computer software. These are important in creating your venue's ambiance. Some of these items are perfect for use in color-changing bars, tables, walls and ceilings.

LEDs

LEDs have decreased in price over the last few years and increased in sophistication and ease of use. Now, you are able to use LEDs in many interesting and creative ways, as they come in so many different styles and formats.

The newest LED innovation are long, thin strips that can be purchased in specified lengths. When positioned inches from each other and in long rows, they create an inexpensive LED video screen. Once, an LED video screen cost millions and now it is at your fingertips for under $10,000.

LEDs come in many formats:
1. Foot-long strips;
2. 1-foot to 4-foot-long tubes;
3. Flat, square panels from 1-foot to 2-foot square;
4. New video-screen format strips;
5. Large outdoor/indoor wash fixtures;
6. Flat strips;
7. LED rope light;
8. MR-16s.

LEDs have become a staple around the world. In bar and nightclub design and development, finding new, creative ways to integrate LEDs has become a passion for some designers who love color and the control that can be found with LEDs. Software and control panels with wireless remotes are used in getting just the right mood set for any area.

LEDs can be linked together to make long runs or elaborate groupings of intelligent, controllable, color-changing effects.

Things you will need for your LEDs:
1. Power supply
2. Mounting clips
3. Software
4. PC and monitor
5. Cat-5 cable
6. LEDs and linking cables

Par 64 with color Scroller

The older way of creating color-changing wash effects was the use of a Par 64 with an attached color Scroller. This was extremely bright but had a short bulb life and lots of moving parts. Color Scrollers still are effective for concerts and nightclubs, but are rarely used for architectural-effects lighting.

Color Scrollers are controlled from your DMX lighting controller, and you will be able to scroll, flash, pulse and blast different colors.

Fiber-optic lights

Fiber-optic lighting has been around for awhile and can create wonderful effects. The most popular is the starry sky effect, with hundreds of twinkling and shining stars in the ceiling. Fiber-optic curtains are also popular, but now have been replaced with LED curtains.

Fiber-optic systems function with a fiber-optic launcher, which is a light source. That then projects light into the end of a bundle of fiber-optic cables. The light travels down the fiber until it is terminated and appears as a shinning speck at the end of the fiber strands.

Fiber-optic launchers can be sophisticated lights with color-changing, dimming and scrolling effects, or they can be a simple, one-color light source.

Things you will need for your fiber optic effect:
1. Fiber-optic launcher or light source
2. Optional controller
3. Bundles of fiber-optic cable
4. Fiber-optic termination points, such as a ceiling or curtain

Lighting controller

When choosing the right lighting controller to handle all of your venue's needs, you will be best advised by the company that is installing and designing the system.

Here are some of the major manufacturers of lighting consoles:
1. Martin Lighting = Light Jockey, Maxxyz
2. Highend = Hog and Hog PC consoles
3. Avolites = Pearl, Sapphire, Diamond
4. Grand MA = Grand MA consoles
5. ALS advanced lighting systems = Enigma
6. ETC = Expression, Acclaim, Obsession

Every intelligent moving lights manufacturer will have a console designed for operating those fixtures. Just remember that every console from the major manufacturers can operate any of the competitor's fixtures. If you have chosen to buy fixtures from one manufacturer and effects from many different companies, you only will need one console to control all of your fixtures, as they all carry the same operating protocol: DMX 512.

How much can I expect to pay for a lighting console?
A good lighting board will cost from $3,600 to $18,000. But I have been using and installing the cost-effective Martin Light Jockey PC system lately, and that will run you, with your PC and flat-panel screen, about $3,600 dollars.

Is a lighting console easy to use?
Yes and no! If you have never touched a lighting console, then it will be all Greek to you, even if it is completely programmed. You will need a trained operator to get you up and running Then, they will be able to train you and your team members on how to use the console.

Who do you recommend I train?
I would teach the management team to turn the console on and off and how to get lighting looks running, But I would hire an experienced lighting tech to operate and program the console for busy nights and weekends.

What do I need in my DJ booth for my lighting guy?
1. One lighting controller
2. One flat-panel, 19-inch monitor
3. Two 20-amp circuit
4. One or two surge-protected power strips
5. A chair or tall bar stool

Attachment points

Do you recall this from the beginning of the design section, reminding you to design to satiate the animal in us all?

When designing, design for the animal!

What does that statement mean? It states that, just like animals, we humans are no different and have similar instincts, desires and needs.

<u>Comfort:</u> *Finding comfort in the animal world can be as easy as needing to kick your dog off of the couch everyday when you get home. No matter how many times you yell at him or spank him, he just loves that spot on the couch!*

Another way for me to describe an attachment point is that it is like a favorite teddy bear or your little blanket when you were a baby. When you didn't have, it you were lost and the whole world would end if you didn't get it back as fast as possible!

"In your comfort zone, you feel safe and secure."

Attaching yourself to an object—any object—can create a feeling of comfort, and all too often, not enough objects of attachment exist in a venue.

<u>What is it in our psyche that creates stage fright or a fear of public speaking?</u>
Do we all have an ingrained suspicion or insecurity that everyone is looking at us and judging or ridiculing us in someway?

When a patron enters a venue, busy or not, they will immediately seek out an attachment point, and the first and most comfortable attachment point is a place to sit. All of the seating you provide are examples of prime attachment points. This type of attachment point is always the first to be filled with customers. You and your designer must figure out how to create and place other types of attachment points throughout the venue.

Too bad you can't just fill your entire venue with furniture! I can just imaging walking into a 3,000-square-foot bar and finding 200 couches and 150 love seats stacked to the roof in order to seat everyone comfortably.

Since seating takes up a large amount of space and cuts down on your flow patterns, you will need to find a balance in choosing your seating styles. The amount of standing or leaning attachment points you develop must not interfere with flow patterns.

Here are some attachment points, from best to worst:
- Booth or couch
- Chair or barstool
- Bar top

- **High-top table**
- **Communal table**
- **Drink rail**
- **Pony wall**
- **Railing**
- **Platform**
- **Structural column**
- **Wall**
- **Air**

- <u>Booths, couches and love seats</u>: These are the best attachment points because of the high level of private, personal space patrons get and the total comfort level. Two people can occupy a booth for four, or a couch, all night, and it is accepted that this area has become a private space for them.
- <u>Chairs and bar stools</u>: Bar stools are the most familiar style of bar seating and offer patrons an individual style of comfortable attachment. Chairs, on the other hand, are more common to dinning areas. Chairs are more mobile than bar stools and allow for diverse seating arrangements.
- <u>Bar top</u>: The amount of attachment points at a bar with bar stools is less than half of a bar without stools. The stool is often the choice of smaller bars and pubs but not nightclubs or high-end lounges. Customer volume will dictate this for every venue.
- <u>High-top tables</u>: These 42-inch-high tables are designed to be placed in a venue's open area, with bar stools for seating. These are tall to keep customers seated at eye level with standing patrons, and are very mobile and functional, with attachment points without seating.
- <u>Communal tables</u>: These are oversized, 42-inch-high tables that can be created in any shape, and should have some bar stools to accompany them while still leaving attachment space for passing patrons. These tables can be curved, rectangle or functional shapes but never square. These may take up too much valuable floor space in smaller venues.
- <u>Drink rails</u>: Great places to consider adding drink rails are along walls, dance-floor perimeters or as flow-pattern designators. Wall-mounted drink rails should not project more than 6 inches from the wall unless you plan to use them for food service. Stand-alone drink rails used as perimeters should be 42 inches high and no more than 6 inches wide, with raised lips on the dance-floor sides to prevent spillage onto the dance floor. Always firmly secure these to the floor, and if need be, add a short right angle at one end for stability.

I recommend you never let patrons drink on the dance floor as spills create hazards and hazards create lawsuits.

- **Pony wall:** This is a short wall that divides rooms or sections off areas. Pony walls should be between 36 inches to 42 inches tall and you should top them in wood, metal or stone if possible to create a drink placement point.
- **Railing:** This is a standard or safety railing and is a great attachment point for patrons, offering a good, secure place to lean onto or to attach to with a 360-degree view. Railings are often meant to keep an area clear or to divide flow patterns and not for attachment so security will often be needed to keep these rails clear of customers.
- **Platform:** These can be dance platforms or performance stages and are not designed as attachment points but end up being just that.
- **Structural columns-** Many venues will have numerous structural columns scattered throughout the space and these can be transformed into great attachment points by adding drink rails or railing. Try keeping the surfaces of the columns smooth. On the lower half avoid placing fabrics below 3 feet.
- **Walls-** I keep picturing a high school dance were the boys are on one side and the girls are on the other and the dance floor is empty. The walls worked then and they still work now.
- **Air-** Insecurities! Air is the worst of all attachment points! Go figure! We have become so self-conscious in our society and have so many insecurities about ourselves that placing any of us even slightly out of our comfort zones will make us extremely uncomfortable.

In other countries, hugging your best friends is completely comfortable, but in the United States, we have developed a wide personal space boundary. In most countries, hugging as a greeting is the norm, and even cheek kisses are common, but in the United States, distance and personal space are the rule.

In the United States, displays of personal affection are limited, and barriers to creating new relationships are higher and harder to breach every day. As people, we are our own worst enemy in the quest for a mate, and our own greatest advocate for loneliness and social dysfunction.

Bar Design

Let's look at an example of how adding some cheap and easy attachment points can add to a venue.

Below, this venue has no flow pattern and has one large, open common area for dancing. The basic fundamentals of the layout are good, with multiple bars, but it still has no flow and fails to supply enough functional attachment points.

Patrons will enter this venue and seek out the most comfortable attachment points first, which will be the seating areas. The major fault here is that the best attachment points are the seating and the bar, which are all on the venue's perimeters, leaving a huge, open, empty area in the center as a void.

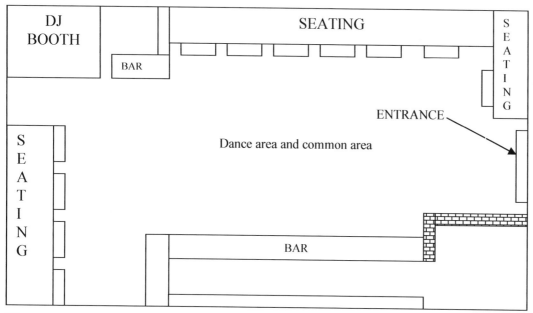

Now, we will add multiple attachment points to this venue, creating flow and filling the void. We will use two communal, 42-inch-high and eight-foot-wide tables with bar stools. Then we will add a dance platform with a railing for go-go dancers and patrons to dance on. You can see that we have created a flow pattern and can easily adjust the communal tables and bar stools to accommodate the dance floor, as they are movable.

Next, we will place a functional art piece in the center of the communal tables to break up the open sight lines and make the space more intimate and not seem so wide open. The art piece only needs to be two to four feet high off or can even hang over the table.

The Little Black Bar Book

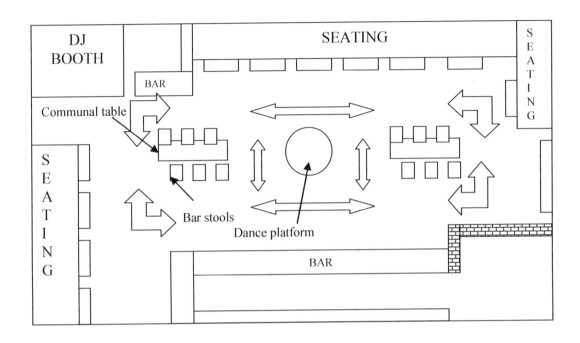

This Pill Allows You to Fly

A man went into a bar in a high-rise. He saw another man take a pill, take a drink, walk to an open window and jump out. He flew around for a minute and zipped back into the bar.

As the amazed newcomer watched, the man repeated this twice more. Finally, the man asked if he could have one of the pills. The flyer said it was his last one. The man offered $500 but to no avail. He made a final offer of $1,000.

The flyer reluctantly gave in, took the cash, surrendered the pill, and turned back to the bar. The man took the pill, took a drink, went to the window and jumped out—only to fall to his death.

The bartender walked over to the flyer at the bar, and wiping a glass, said, "You sure are mean when you're drunk, Superman."

Equipment

Let's look at some important items that will help you maintain a smoothly operating business. These items are necessary for day-to-day operations and must be kept in good working order.

You will find that the cost of new equipment is very high. I often prefer to buy items from venues that are in the process of closing or have closed. You can save a huge sum of money on bar and kitchen equipment this way. Bar and kitchen equipment have few moving parts so you will find that used equipment will function just as well as new equipment, often only needing a good cleaning and a few small repairs.

You might consider leasing or buying new bar coolers, freezers and ice machines. These are the key components to quickly delivering cold beverages across your bar. These items must be regularly serviced and closely monitored. If at all possible, have two ice machines in every venue as they are fickle and tend to break down only when you need them the most, such as Saturday night at 11 p.m.

I prefer to lease one new 1,200-pound ice machine and purchase an older, small 600-pound machine as my backup. This will always ensure that I will have the minimum ice needed to get by on a weekend.

As for bar coolers, there are three kinds I prefer to use, and if you are able to buy them used and in somewhat good condition, that is great.

- Top-loading coolers: These are for under your front bar countertop and open and close with a top side-sliding door for easy access. These are faster to access than the back bar cooler, and one should be located next to every well on the left side.
- Back bar cooler: These are the coolers under the back counter, behind the bartenders. They often have glass doors for display purposes. These are great cold storage of beer and chilled liquors.
- Stand-up coolers: These are the type you see at a 7-Eleven or a deli, a tall version of the back bar cooler with sliding glass doors. I prefer to use this type of cooler in most of my venues as the amount of cold storage and quality of display you get is huge, along with the ease of use for bartenders who don't have to bend down and twist to get beer from the lower back-bar coolers. These also can be stocked from the rear in some cases if you position them in front of a storage area. This is very convenient.

Sometimes, you will be taking over an existing business that will have equipment in place, and sometimes you will need to start from scratch. Here are some questions you might need to address:

- What equipment do you already have?
- Is your equipment new or used?
- What equipment do you need?
- What type of maintenance will your equipment require?
- How many wells can you fit behind your bars?
- How many bars will your concept have?
- What type of products will be the prime products sold at your concept?
- What type of specialty equipment is needed for your concept? (i.e. draught beer system.)

Stocking Cold Items/Cold Storage Questions

- What types of products do you use? Twelve-ounce beer, 16 ounce, 40 ounce or draught?
- Do you mostly serve beer or liquor? Beer will need cooler space and liquor will need more ice capacity.
- How big is your venue and do you have room for lots of cold storage units?
- What type of volume of cold beverages will you go through? If you go through 50 cases of beer a night, then you should have cold storage units for 80 percent of that at a minimum.
- How hard is it for you to restock and rotate beer in a cooler unit? You should rotate beer from the bottom of top-loading coolers to the top and from the back of back bar coolers to the front, allowing the newly stocked warm beer time to cool.

What is the minimum cooling time for beer and what is the ideal temperature?
   Different-sized products and the temperatures they are stored at will produce different cooling times. A cold beer should be chilled to 21 degrees and served at 31 degrees max.

JOKE
A man walks into a bar and orders a 12-year-old scotch. The bartender, believing that the customer will not be able to tell the difference, pours him a shot of the cheap 3-year-old house scotch that has been poured into an empty bottle of the good stuff.
The man takes a sip and spits the scotch out on the bar and reams the bartender. "This is the cheapest 3-year-old scotch you can buy. I'm not paying for it. Now, give me a good 12-year-old scotch."
The bartender, now feeling a bit of a challenge, pours him a scotch of much better quality, 6-year-old scotch. The man takes a sip and spits it out on the bar. "This is only 6-year-old scotch. I won't pay for this, and I insist on, a good, 12-year-old scotch."
The bartender finally relents and serves the man his best quality, 12-year-old scotch.
An old drunk from the end of the bar, who has witnessed the entire episode, walks down to the finicky scotch drinker and sets a glass down in front of him and asks, "What do you

think of this?"
The scotch expert takes a sip, and in disgust, violently spits out the liquid yelling "Why, this tastes like piss,"

The old drunk replies, "That's right, now tell me how old I am."

POS Systems

What Software and Point of Sale System Will You Use?

I strongly recommend you use one of the new computerized systems. if at all possible. This will let you track your inventory and sales instantly. A good POS system will not only track sales, but also will keep track of hundreds of different parameters, such as inventory by brand, drink types and promotional items. This tracking can be done hourly, weekly, monthly or annually.

I am most impressed with the Aloha system's ease of use and cost-effectiveness. There are numerous systems to choose from, and most of the newer systems are able to handle any sized operation in the bar and nightclub industry.

A good system will have a main server in the office and touch-screen panels with cash drawers throughout the venue for bartenders, cocktails and cover charges. New POS systems let you monitor all of these stations simultaneously. This will make the lives of your management team much easier, and the peace of mind for investors and owners will be well worth the price you have paid for the system.

Cash registers! These are a cost-effective solution but should be the last resort, as there is no way to track or confirm anything. These might be used for taking cover charges or at the coat check, but are very unreliable and hard to accurately track sales. Security is also a big concern when dealing with employee theft.

Lessons Learned

The first nightclub I was a partner in was Club Freedom in Tempe, Arizona. We were three young guys with little or no investment capital and a dying club based on one night of international DJs. We could only afford cash registers and we paid for it every night with rampant theft from the staff. Employees were not ringing in drinks, stuffing their tip jars, bringing their own bottles into the bar and killing us. We had three separate bars and one overworked general manager to monitor all of them.

I felt like a two-dollar hooker getting a quarter for a full night's work. And just as sore in particular areas, as we were getting fucked hard by everyone. This was my first venture into ownership and was a great learning experience.

POS systems available on the market are:
1. Aloha;
2. Micros;
3. Bar Soft;
4. PCAmerica.com;
5. RestaurantPOS.com

Basic Bar Equipment and Items

All of your equipment should be NSF-certified. These are manufacturing standards set by the National Sanitation Foundation. This rating is accepted by all health departments across the country.

So, let's have a quick look at what bartenders actually need:

- Speed wells (provide fast, easy access to the most commonly used liquors);
- Glassware or cups;
- POS system;
- Ice well;
- Sink;
- Beer taps;
- Soda gun;
- Juices and storm pourers;
- Cocktail equipment (shakers, spinal mixer, hawthorn strainer, bar spoon, sifter, blender, knife, cutting Board, muddling stick and anything else your bar may use);
- Cocktail and drink-garnish containers;
- Cold beer storage;
- Wines;
- Well and premium liquors;
- Straws and napkins;
- Bar towels;
- Trash cans;
- Rubber bar mats.

Bars need to have a back station normally hidden from customers.

- Dishwasher;
- Ice machine;
- Spare equipment and accessories;
- Glassware and cup storage;
- Cleaning materials.

The first stage in designing a bar is simply working out what needs to go where:

- Beer taps and glasses;
- Cocktail equipment, cocktail glasses, cocktail garnishes; Ice well, speed well, straws, coasters, napkins, juices, soda gun and sink;
- Wine and wine glasses;
- Champagne and Champagne glasses.

"It all seems pretty simple but most bars still get it wrong."

Speed and Service

Next, we should think about service. It is important that all drinks are made in front of the guest. The exception, of course, is if you are a service bar that only looks after cocktail waitresses.

With the exception of wine, which I feel is beneficial for guests to see, all the drink-mixing equipment and glassware should be on the service side of the bar.

I feel the beer taps should be shared between bartender stations. This is also because of cost. So it's just now just a matter of laying out the other equipment to best utilize space on the front bar, being mindful not to clutter the bar top so it is easy to keep clean for guests.

The back bar should house most of your bar's premium liquors and coolers storing beer. The placement of your liquor and cold beer storage should be set up so bartenders don't take more than two steps to any item. The only exception is premium liquors that rarely get used and are located on a back display shelf.

The POS system is normally situated directly behind the bartender's ice well on the back bar for efficient access.

The goal of your bar design should be to make bartending functional and efficient so your bartenders can serve more customers in a shorter period of time.

Back Bar Glass Cooler   **Top Loading Cooler**   **Deli Style Cooler**

The Birth of a Bar or Nightclub

This section is aimed at covering some of the main components of a business plan, and to help you succeed as not just a bar but as a business.

A Successful Bar is a Successful Business

Some bars may be successful with educated guess work and lots of luck but most are bound to fail. In this section, my goal is to establish some simple business planning, as it is incredibly important when starting a bar that you are planning for the future success of your venue.

It is important to remember that you are not just opening a bar but operating a business. The first priority is to do extensive research into the local bar and nightclub market. You should look to see if a need is there and if the client base is willing to make the move to the new hot spot in town. You can then develop the concept for filling the available. The next step is to develop a rough draft of a business plan, even if you are not raising money for the project.

SUMMARY TIME

This summary is an overview of your business. Do this with the help of experienced professionals.

Summary Contents
- Brief description of your bar or nightclub concept
- Business motives
- Brief outline of your bar or nightclub strategies
- Your concepts for targeting markets and demographics
- Finances required/budget outline
- Financial projections
- Best- and worst-case scenarios with an exit strategy

The Business Concept

This is a key component because it represents your vision of your bar or nightclub.
- What type of bar or club will your business be?
- Where will it be located?
- What is your vision?
- Why will it be unique?

I recommend setting goals for each key component of your business. For example: how much food/liquor/beer do you expect to sell each week or month? For instance, if you want to net $25,000 per week, you will need $100,000 in gross weekly sales with a return of 25 percent. Some bars and clubs generate a 30 percent return for years strictly from a good cover charge.

Next, it's important to list each service you will provide and a detailed description of what they are. Then list the advantages you have over your competition. How is what you offer better service, food, entertainment or experience than what the public is already getting elsewhere?

LEGAL & ADMINISTRATIVE REQUIREMENTS

Get a lawyer from the very beginning to help you set up the operating agreement and all or any contracts with your partners. And, find one who specializes in liquor license law for the state, county or city in which you are planning to open your establishment.

The cost for lawyer's fees for the liquor license will range from $5,000 to $8,000, depending on what and how many licenses you need. Some states require separate beer, wine and liquor licenses. When it comes to a gaming license, the cost and difficulty will climb.

Don't be afraid to ask other bar owners who they used and how much it cost. They will often help you. If not, look in the Yellow Pages or consult the local legal bar association.

As for the lease, it is a good idea to have a lawyer review the lease. Deal with the owner directly and you will save each other a lot of time and money in legal fees. This also will help you build a rapport with your landlord.

- <u>What will be your bar's name?</u> You will want to search the local area to make sure the name is not already taken. Be creative; don't just steal another bar's name or concept completely. I have been in the middle of many discussions regarding the ethics of stealing ideals from another concept. You will need to register with your local Secretary of State.
- <u>What will be your legal structure?</u> It is a good idea to open as a limited liability company or LLC. This will protect the owners and investors from personal lawsuits.
- <u>What is your bar's legal and tax implications?</u>
- <u>Do you have any business restrictions, requirements or regulations, either locally, state or federally?</u> Often, you must look into local restrictions on building a bar or club as there may be guidelines or restrictions for such issues as proximity to churches or other bars and clubs

- **Do you have all of the needed contracts?** You will need an operating agreement signed by all the partners first and foremost. Then you will need to get contracts with your management team, as well as nondisclosure agreements.
- **What kind of insurance do you require?** Wow, this is a big nut to crack! This is often based on sales and is never a cheap bill—sometimes up to and over $100,000. Most bars will run you $30,000 to $70,000 per year. You should always get at least $1 million in blanket coverage. One extremely important clause that must be in your policy is the strike clause. This covers you if your employees get into a fistfight and are forced to strike a patron for any reason. Some policies will not cover fights so be sure you have that covered.

BUSINESS FINANCIAL PLANNING

The bar and nightclub business is one of high risk and high rate of return, or ROI, and the chance to make 15 percent to 30 percent on your investment is enough of a motivation for some to take the risks. The idea of having returns on your investment within the first 90 days also is quite appealing.

When entering the bar and nightclub business, having the right goals in mind from the beginning is a must. Many operators and investors are looking to use this venture as a tool to be young again, get girls and party.

Story

In 2006, I was hired to consult for a group opening a bar on the Las Vegas Strip. The group consisted of one of the owners, the main financial investor and a third partner, the so-called promotions expert. From the first meeting, I really enjoyed the main investor's attitude and understanding of the need to focus on creating a successful, profit-generating venue.

Once I was introduced to the promotions partner, red flags immediately went off. I couldn't understand why he had been brought in to collaborate on this project. As a paid consultant, I soon came to realize that this was going to be a nightmare with false promises and bullshit handed out on a huge scale.

Here, the promotions expert's lack of understanding and unwillingness to listen to professional advice would cost over a $1 million in losses.

The investor and the promotions expert had no real experience in the bar business, and the promotions expert was only trying to hook up with the staff and pay for his drug and *gambling habits with an overblown salary of $10,000 per month and a large percentage of ownership.*

The promotional expert was creating a job for himself and making a career move, but he was unable to pull this off. The bar quickly failed because of a lack of understanding and leadership.

The promotional expert was informed throughout the entire project by experienced operators and consultants numerous times on how to correctly perform the tasks needed to create a successful concept.

The poor investor was warned many times about his choice of a partner who continued to blame everything on everyone else until there was no one left but bill collectors!

Establishing Costs and the Sourcing of Funds for Opening Related Expenses

Figuring out the costs associated with your coming operation can be figured out with the help of your local distributors and purveyors, who will provide you with spread sheets of costs: your lease, labor, beer, liquor and soft goods such as napkins, glassware, plastic cups, etc.

Your lease payment and local labor rates for tipped employees must be researched in order to get your labor costs correct.

Your concept's source of funds to pay for inventory can be put on credit with local distributors, allowing 30 days to pay. Local distributors will have credit applications for you to fill out and return to figure out the amount of credit available.

For your first opening order, many distributors and the lines they represent will provide you with big discounts and offers, such as donated liquor for your opening parties. You should take advantage of these specials and free offers that come with no strings attached.

Sponsorship packages are available from most vendors and should be taken advantage of through direct negotiations. Products and services can be donated or given at huge discounts (such as two-for-one) to help offset opening costs.

Below is a list of vendors that have been extremely giving:
1. Anheuser Busch, up to $150,000
2. RJ Reynolds Tobacco, up to $30,000
3. Skyy Vodka
4. Red Bull, up to $30,000
5. X-Rated Vodka, up to $16,000

6. Rockstar energy drink
7. Miller Brewing Company, up to $100,000

Some of these vendors have given from $5,000 up to $150,000 to different concepts. It is always worth asking for. Have a sponsorship package put together. Let them know what your concept is and how their products fit into it and why they will be huge sellers, along with advertisement locations in and outside of your venue.

Signing an exclusive deal with these vendors for up to one year and only carrying their products is to be expected in any deal

Equipment Leasing

Another way to mitigate the output of investment dollars is to lease equipment. There are many companies that will do large-scale equipment leases for new bars and nightclubs. You can save yourself tens of thousands of dollars in capital for other uses by leasing new equipment, and at the same time, have new equipment for your concept.

Analysis and Creation of Financial Tables

As part of your financial plan, you should break down your monthly outgoing expenses into monthly or weekly tables. These tables should include all the costs associated with operations, your vendors, distributors and the monthly labor costs.

These tables will give you a good overview in the form of a quick-look P&L. You should develop these tables pre-opening and use them as guidelines for the first six months of operation. You will need time to get a good grasp of your true operational costs associated with a new concept.

Often, when figuring out pre-opening financial tables, you should inflate your outgoing expenses by 20% you will have extra inventory in stock just in case you underestimated your concept. You will always use this stock at some point, and if you have the storage room available, the extra stock will not sit for long.

A Very Depressed Man

There's a man sitting at a bar just looking at his drink. He stays like that for half an hour. Then, a big, trouble-making truck driver steps next to him, takes the drink from the guy and just drinks it all down.
The poor man starts crying. The truck driver says, "Come on, man, I was just joking. Here, I'll buy you another drink. I just can't stand seeing a man crying."

"No, it's not that. This day is the worst of my life. First, I slept in and I was late to my office. My boss, in an outrage, fired me. When I left the building to my car, I found out it was stolen. The police said they could do nothing. I got a cab to return home and when I got out, I
remembered I left my wallet and credit cards on the seat but the cab driver just drove away. I went home and when I got there, I found my wife sleeping with the gardener. I left home and came to this bar. And while I was thinking about putting an end to my life, you showed up and drank my poison."

STAFFING

In the beginning of every venue's life, you must over-hire! During your opening, your venue will be overstaffed by as much as 30 percent! This will allow you to cut out the undesirables, underachievers and drama queens during the training and pre-opening phases of opening.

During your first weeks, you will be able to find out who on your team are going to be team players who will help you kick ass!

You will be looking for employees displaying dedication, devotion, skill sets and the willingness to put in extra hours helping with opening-related activities, such as stocking and inventory. Team members who help with cleaning or repairing items in the bar or nightclub are showing they want to be a part of the team.

You need to look for team members who display winning personalities, delivering energy and excitement with their servicing skills. These staff members can be quick with a joke or have a knack for remembering names and faces.

An employee's ability to try to integrate new abilities and skills such as flair bartending (which is juggling bottles and shaker cups) is always a plus and shows a dedication to the position.

You will quickly find out who is going to be trouble, and in the industry, "drama" is a bad word. These employees are never happy and always seem to be complaining about something or someone. They will never be happy and must be quickly removed from your business.

Your team is your new family and troublesome children have no place in it. Once you have identified and fired the drama queens, the remaining members of your team will function much better. You must quickly discover which employees work well with others, as some have strengths and weaknesses that can be balanced out with the team working together.

How Do You Approach Staff Recruitment and Hiring?

The secret of good staff recruitment is to hire key members from local hot-spots in town. I like to hire well-known and experienced employees of other popular bars and nightclubs in the local area.

Popular and skilled bar staff are always looking to move to the newest, hottest location to make easy money.

This works many ways, as I love to hire top talent from the local competition well in advance of opening. This is the best and fastest way to promote to the in-crowd. These new employees will be spreading the word to all of their customers and friends that they will be working at that new hot bar or nightclub opening soon. They are selling your venue by creating buzz and hyping up the local in-crowd.

I will often release limited information to team members on what will make the bar or nightclub stand apart from other venues, such as, "We will have stripper poles or a sex swing," or "all the girls will wear little, naughty school-girl outfits," or the best one, "the owners are from Vegas." This one is funny to me how well it actually works!

The Fox and the Hound

One example of this is by taking two bartenders, one with great skills and one new to the business. By putting the new bartender next to the veteran who might be a little jaded but who has skill, speed, mixology knowledge and experience, the new bartender will learn faster.

The new bartender will eventually pick up the skill sets from working with the more experienced bartender, and both will rely on each other to maximize service and speed in order to maximize guest tips.

How Do I Staff?

Often, you will get hundreds, if not thousands, of applicants showing up for every position, from bathroom attendant and bar back to management. The hours you will spend interviewing possible candidates will be long and difficult. You will need to make hundreds of appointments and callbacks to narrow down your potential team members.

Always take a Polaroid picture of every applicant and staple it to the job application or resume. This will help you place a name and face to the individuals in your huge stack of applications.

Hundreds of qualified professionals will apply and you will need to ask them what they can bring to the venue and how they think they will fit into the picture.

You will need to begin figuring out how many staff members you need.
- What are your hours of operation?
- How many days will you be open?
- How many shifts will you run per day?
- How many bars will you need to staff?
- How many exits and entrances will you need to cover with security?
- How large is your venue?

- How many cocktail sections will you have?
- How many bathroom attendants will you have?
- Who will fill your management positions: bar manager, head of security, assistant manager and general manager?
- Management shifts must include weekday and weekend daytime operations.
- Where will your cleaning crew be outsourced?
- Who will be your daytime bookkeeper?

How Many Employees do I Hire?

Once you have answered the above questions, you will need to do a mock schedule with fake names. Then, overstaff every position by 20 percent. This will cover you for no-shows and team members you will need to let go.

For example, say you have six bartenders on one shift and six wells or serving locations behind your bars. In the first 30 days of operation, you should have seven or eight bartenders behind the bars. Yes, they will be on top of each other, but you can give them 30-minute breaks as the night continues to keep the numbers down behind the bar. This will give you a good chance to see them all work together in a stress-filled environment.

The ones who can work well with others will not have a problem. This is the heart of your operation and needs to function efficiently.

"The bar top is one big ATM, and every dollar that comes across that bar goes into your pocket. You must make every transaction quick and easy.

The number of employees you hire will detrimentally impact both the quality of the speed and service of your concept. A professional sports team having the best players always helps, and you will need the best tools to make your business successful.

Overstaffing Pros and Cons

- **Employees such as Bussers, BarBacks and Security make less money in tips as the number of employees grows;**
- Bartenders have to divide tips between more bartenders;
- Cocktails have smaller sections and less patrons;
- Security-guard payroll is much higher;
- Managers are more relaxed and focused, and there is less burnout;
- Customer appreciation for quick service;
- The balancing act! Happy Staff< > Happy Patrons

Overstaffing will lead to lots of complaints from your staff. You need to make it clear that you are over-scheduling on purpose to find out who and how many staff you need to provide high-quality service and meet the daily sales numbers needed.

Adjust the schedule as the team members begin to work together as an efficient team. You also are creating a team-based and efficient workplace.

Quote to Staff

If the bar can still ring $15,000 on a Saturday night with five bartenders not sacrificing the quality of service, then you will drop the number to five, but not until the time that management feels comfortable. The bar staff will continue at six or seven bartenders every Saturday night."

Financial Monitoring

It is important to hire a professional bookkeeper, accountant and knowledgeable management team who will be able to monitor, track and forecast the incoming and outgoing expenses and sales goals. A good bar manager will have a strong grasp of day-to-day operations. Monthly liquor-cost reports will help keep you operating in the median range of 17 percent to 21 percent.

This will guarantee things are on track, and as long as you keep within these parameters, you will be able to base sales and profit projections on your monthly estimated sales.

Monthly profit and loss reports should come from your bookkeeper and management team working together to control and monitor outgoing expenses and related operating costs.

It is important for your management team to evaluate possible threats from employees to your cash flow from theft and lack of performance.

Good examples of losses in bars are theft, waste and excessive comp tabs (the number of free drinks team members give to their friends and patrons). A plan needs to be in place for these potential problems, such as the implementation of drink tickets and mandatory receipts for every transaction. These systems will in no way stop theft. They are put in place so if you do catch someone stealing, they understand the procedures and that not following them is a clear case of theft, which means an instant termination from employment.

Waste, spill tabs and breakage forms need to be in place for the team members at each bar. Should these incidents occur, a record needs to be made of each and every occurrence.

Keeping track of your business is important to your success, and having good people in place and a trustworthy team are the keys to a profitable and well-run concept."

JOKE

An Englishman, an Irishman and a Scotsman walk into a bar and each order a pint of beer. When the drinks arrive they notice that all three pints have a fly in them.
The Englishman just looks at his pint in disgust and pushes it away.
The Irishman picks out the fly with his fingers, throws it on the floor and proceeds to drink his beer.
The Scotsman picks the fly out of his pint, and holds it over the drinking saying, "Come on you little git, spit it out!"

TRAINING

How Do I Train My Team?

Some people think that training bar and nightclub staff is done be hiring some people with experience and then throwing them behind the bar.

This is not the right way to train your team members. You need to match your concept with your team training, remembering that most experienced servers and bartenders have both good and bad habits from their last jobs and that you need to train out the bad habits.

One of the most important fundamentals of training that I find missing is general workspace monitoring.

Here are a few examples of general workspace monitoring:
- Stocking par levels of glassware, liquor, beer and ice;
- Keeping the immediate work area clean, both the bar top and behind the bar;
- Keeping floors clear of debris;
- Making sure that beer is rotated from the back of the cooler to the front, or from bottom to top, and that your team is not selling warm beer.

Here are some of the things that are a must in training:
- You must train a smile onto every team member'
- Greetings are extremely important, and touching is the most powerful greeting of all! Handshakes, hugs and cheek kisses are a must from every team member to one another and to every customer all night. Don't be afraid to pat someone on the back or hug patrons every time you greet them.
- Vocal greetings are great from over the bar, but remember not to use the same one for every guest. Be creative. Make them feel like a customer, not another cow in the herd. Try to identify regular patrons and remember their names.
- As soon as you can get the team behind the actual bars and get them comfortable with where everything is located, have them help with stocking and setting up the bar.
- Drink specials, such as creative signature drinks, are popular in lounges but often forgotten after the first few weeks—if they were ever learned at all.
- The presentation of team members, including uniforms and general appearance. If you are going to open a rock 'n' roll bar, tattoos and wild hair styles are a plus as they will give your bar more character . I have

allowed vulgar T-shirts on male staff in my establishments and they caused quite a stir, to say the least, with the landlord and patrons. The bar backs wore "MILF Hunter" T-shirts in one of my rock 'n' roll venues.
- Staff and management drinking—wow, what a can of worms this is! My attorney has advised me to say, "At no time is it acceptable for any employee to consume alcohol while at work or on the premises. Any employee caught drinking will be given a written warning and sent home. Upon a second incident, they will be terminated." Well, let's just say that I don't promote it but do not condone it, either. Just remember, everything has its limits and your team members must understand this.

How to Motivate Your Team to Upsell!

The easy point to make to your team members is that people tip an average of 20 percent on the check, and the higher their sales are, the more they should be making in tips.

A provocative way to tackle this is to have an end-of-day total-sales competition with bonuses, cash prizes and giveaways. This can be done with the different positions, such as bartenders vs. bartenders and servers vs. servers.

A happy team is one that is making money. You or your GM need to be able to act as the captain of the ship by leading, motivating and guiding your team. Be aware of your team members' misgivings and strengths, and take advantage of these. Team up staff by placing motivated members with others who are not so motivated to see if the motivated member can transfer knowledge and skill sets on to the weaker team member.

Contact your distributors and vendors and ask them to help you motivate your team. Distributors and brands will have programs to help you with training, rewards and incentives.

How Do I Separate People From Their Money?

This is your team members' job, and with proper training, this will become easy. Men cannot resist a beautiful cocktail waitress in a cute uniform who always pitches the upsell to them from well to premium.

You can work with your distributors to get discount pricing based on volume and case orders. These become your specials and become the team members' promotional pitches, with incentives from the liquor or beer company.

Customer: "Give me a Red Bull vodka."
Bartender: "How about I make that a Grey Goose for you?"

Customer: "Sure."

Three customers come into your bar and sit at a table. Your server approaches them.

Server: "Welcome to Stingray's Bar and Grill, guys! How are you today?"
Customer 1: "Great."
Server: "Just to let you know, we have Bud Light pitchers and Corona buckets on special. What can I get you?"
Customer 1: "What do you think, guys? Corona or Bud?"
Customer 2: "Bud's great!"
Server: "Perfect! I'll be right back."

A server's greeting, attitude, and attention to service and details are the most critical points of contact between your venue and your patrons. This makes the training, hiring and motivation all critical elements of a successful concept.

Making the Guest Feel the Love

Patrons must feel the love, starting with the door hosts. In the training manual section of this book, we have gone over the importance of the greeting, and now I will tell you how important human-to-human contact and identification is in the bar and nightclub business and in life.

Try hugging someone, even a stranger, when you first encounter them in a social situation. The impact is huge as we are a culture taught to defend our personal space to the death. Its funny how we want to get naked with the first hot chick we see but we wouldn't hug that girl when we first meet her! This doesn't make sense! You want to have sex with her but you don't want to hug her?!

How do you feel when you actually get an honest greeting from someone instead of the fake "welcome to McDonald's" bullshit we deal with everyday? You almost can't tell the difference nowadays!

Be different. Try to drop your 2 ½-foot barrier of personal space and give someone a hug, for Christ's sake. You need to lead your team by example, and they need to lead your patrons by example.

Look for this in your team members and reward them. If you are watching your team and you witness these random acts of kindness, reward that employee on the spot with $20. This is positive reinforcement, and will eventually transfer into their everyday actions, and those actions will become automatic when they are at work.

Training Manuals—What They Do and Who They Are For

Training manuals should be an extended version of the standard operating procedures for each employee, detailing what they need to know to perform their position, including their duties and obligations.

Training manuals are often a waste of paper and time if you are hiring a team that has no experience, or with no knowledge of the position they are hired for.

"Hiring inexperienced staff for key positions is never a good idea."

Here are some of the key positions outlined in training manuals:
- Bartender
- Cocktail waitress
- Bar back
- Security

The basic training manual goes over the standard legal needs for any bar. Here are some important items to add and review with your team in your training manual:

- <u>Sexual harassment</u>: This is the most critical issue for all bars and nightclubs. I highly recommend looking into hiring a local consultant who will come into the venue and give a short class to the whole team. This will cover your butt big-time.
- <u>Consequences</u>: This is needed to let employees know the punishments for failing to perform or show up for shifts are serious, and that they will be given a written warning or terminated for these offences.
- <u>Underage service</u>: It is important to cover the requirements of your liquor license. Let the employees know that even if a patron gets past the door but does not appear to be of legal age, they still should ID that patron if they have any doubt.
- <u>No-strike policy</u>: This is especially important for the security team, but includes all team members and managers. Team members are never allowed to strike a patron! Security team members need to restrain and remove unruly patrons. Your heads of security and management should have procedures in place for any altercation or disturbance. Every altercation must be followed up with a written report.

I Didn't Get Any Money This Time
A man in a bar sees a friend at a table, drinking by himself. Approaching the friend, he comments, "You look terrible. What's the problem?"
"My mother died in August," the friend says, "and left me $25,000."

"Gee, that's tough," he replies.
"Then in September," the friend continues, "My father died, leaving me $90,000."
"Wow! Two parents gone in two months! No wonder you're depressed."
"And last month, my aunt died and left me $15,000."
"Three close family members lost in three months? How sad."
"Then this month," continues the friend, "absolutely nothing!"

Security

What makes a good security team

Brawn **Head of Security** **Front-Door Hosts**

Do's and Don'ts for Your Security Team

Let's look at some items for your security training manual:
1- Never strike a patron for any reason. Subdue and remove them.

In situations where an altercation occurs, patrons are most likely drunk and belligerent. Taking this into account, you should always remember that they are doing what you want them to do: spending lots of money in your bar. Some just don't understand their limits and tend to overdo it.

Security should be trained to restrain and remove patrons without punching or striking them in anyway. This should be done in pairs by security. This guarantees there is always a witness.

2- Security team and all team members should defend their personal safety at all times.

Having been involved with and witnessed out-of-control bar fights, I recommend that all team members be trained to exit quickly and defend themselves at all times with equal or greater force.

3- Security situations should always be handled in pairs.

This is important for many reasons. If patrons are having a dispute, then pairs of security should handle the situation immediately. Pairs of security should act quickly to safeguard a customer's safety. This insures the safety of the security team and mitigates the bar's liability. An overwhelming show of force is often a great deterrent to violent behavior.

4- Preventative security is the best security.

The best security is always preventative and proactive. Being unable to identify potential problems before they occur is often the failing of many security team members.

Let me give you an example of how to handle a potential problem:

You identify a patron intoxicated who is starting to get a little loud and bothersome to other customers. Security or management backed by security should approach the guest and kindly ask him to step aside just for a second,. This should be out of the public area.

This removes him from his friends and any need to show off or display any bravado. Once removed, explain to him that you are concerned for him, then send a security guard to get him a cold bottle of water. This shows him you are trying to help and are only concerned for their welfare. At this time, you should make the call on letting him stay or calling him a cab.

Never just throw the patron out. This will separate you from bad operators. Once you thrown a patron out, you leave them with few options, and one of those options is to drive home drunk.

5- Altercation removal procedure

This is important for many reasons. If two patrons are having a dispute, one pair of security should remove one of the customers to a predetermined safe zone away from public areas, while the other pair of security removes the other patron to a separate safe zone. The immediate removal of the patrons from the public area is a must.

Plans for removal should be set up beforehand, outlining exit strategies and safe zones for removal when altercations occur. Never take an altercation out the front entryway. This will always turn into a circus, with lots of yelling and bullshit because you have now added an audience to your problem.

Always file an in-house report, make photocopies of IDs, record all contact information, take statements if necessary, and contact the local police department if needed.

6- Identifying regular drunks and trouble makers.

Front-door security should be aware of chronic trouble-makers, and if needed, refuse them entry. This is important and healthy for the venue's overall operation. You have the right to refuse service to anyone!

7- Staffing correctly.

In the beginning, overstaffing is a good idea for many reasons as it sets the tone for your establishment in the eyes of the public. Having an overwhelming security presence from day one will send a clear message to patrons that you are taking security seriously. I recommend hiring a female security guard as they are so often underestimated in defusing situations. No one wants to punch a girl! A female security team member will take the sails out of a drunken male patron fast.

Bartender

Here is a good example of what a good bartender training manual should include:

Bartender Responsibilities
- Stocking (beer, liquor, cups, ice)
- Immediate area management (cleaning, awareness)
- Inventory management (beginning and end of night)
- Drink knowledge
- ABC (alcohol beverage control) is a state agency, and all employees who handle alcohol will need to have attended classes and be certified. You might be able to have a certified teacher come to your bar or nightclub and train all of your team in one short class. It is preferable for the owner to pay for the teacher in this instance.

Bartender Basics
- Smile, have fun and have a personality!
- Creative greetings, including hugs!
- Make good drinks fast and don't over pour!
- Keep your area clean!
- Learn to recognize regulars.
- Don't steal or I will feed you to the fishes!
- Learn the specialty drink list and menu.

- Personal hygiene, please.
- Boyfriend/girlfriend patronage = no drama.
- Drink procedures for family and friends; this includes complementary tabs.

"Keep your training manual short and simple!"

<u>Some common sense for your team to understand in your training manuals:</u>
- If a glass breaks near an ice well, they need to pour cranberry juice over the ice immediately. Then burn the ice and wipe out the well. If they don't understand the importance of this, they may have never worked in a bar before and need more training before they are allowed to work in your venue.
- No-showing and no-calling on a shift means possible termination.
- **It is important for your team members and management team to fully understand your concept. Your team must be able to execute the ideas and principal aspects of your concept flawlessly.**

<u>Bartender</u>
What is the difference between a nightclub bartender and a bar bartender? Answer: customer interaction time. Bar bartenders have a longer period of time between guests, which allows for more interaction.

<u>Lounge training</u>: Lounges need to focus on attentive service.

<u>Table hostess:</u> This position is the main point of interest in many lounges, with bottle and table service so popular and in high demand in many major metropolitan areas. A well-trained table hostess will keep high-dollar patrons coming back over and over again. Table displays and presentation, along with up-selling, are a must in training new table hostesses.

<u>Door host:</u> This position is important as the host needs to identify VIPs and accommodate the needs of female patrons quickly and diplomatically. Good hosts can insure quick, escorted entry from the door to a reserved table for guests. Greetings from hosts are important, and don't forget the hugs! Remembering and identifying repeat customers and name recollection is crucial. Humor and patience also are important virtues.

<u>Nightclub training</u>: Nightclubs need to focus on speed of service.
<u>Bartender:</u> This position is often the main point of interest, with large numbers of patrons requiring a high volume of drinks in a short span of time. Bartenders also must manage the needs of busy cocktail stations.

Security: This position is often busy with the large number of patrons and the large number of issues arising out of the volume. The security team manager needs to manage security issues, prioritizing security risks as they occur. Security team members need to take a preventative stance and proactively protect patrons. The security door team needs to address possible risky customers before they are allowed to enter the venue.

Cocktail Servers: This position is difficult. With the density of patrons, cocktail servers will be fighting the crowds to get drinks from the service well to customers. Cocktail servers must learn to create pathways from the service well to their stations. This goes back to your initial bar design. A poor design will hinder your sales figures.

Bar/Pub Training: Bars and pubs need to focus on identity.

Bartender: This position is the ambassador of the bar, injecting soul and personality into the venue as the bartender will have more time to interact with patrons. This position needs to identify customers' names and their common drinks of choice. They need to introduce and educate patrons on new ethnic beers, drinks and the venue's customs. Greetings are a must, and don't forget the hugs!

Cocktail/food server: This position requires a combination of liquor and food knowledge. During the early hours of operation, food will be in higher demand. Later, liquor and beer will be the staples. This position will have longer hours of operation than most nightclubs, with both slow- and high-volume periods each day. This position should be able to identify regulars and promote new menu items and daily specials. Don't forget the hugs!

Joke

Consultants—you've just gotta love them!

A timeless lesson on how consultants can make a difference for an organization ...

Last week, we took some friends out to a new restaurant, and noticed that our waiter was carrying a spoon in his shirt pocket. It seemed a little strange, but I ignored it.

However, when the busboy brought out water and utensils, I noticed he also had a spoon in his shirt pocket. Then, I looked around the room and saw that all of the staff had spoons in their pockets. When the waiter came back to serve our soup, I asked, "Why the spoon?"

"Well," he explained, "the restaurant's owners hired Anderson Consulting, efficiency experts , in order to revamp all of our processes. After several months of statistical analysis, they concluded that customers drop their spoons 73.84 percent more often than any other utensil. This represents a drop frequency of approximately 3 spoons per table per hour. If

our personnel are prepared to deal with that contingency, we can reduce the number of trips back to the kitchen and save 15 man-hours per shift."

As luck would have it, I dropped my spoon and he was able to replace it with his spare spoon. "I'll get another spoon next time I go to the kitchen instead of making an extra trip to get it right now." I was rather impressed.

The waiter served our main course and I continued to look around. I then noticed that there was a very thin string hanging out of the waiter's fly. Looking around, I noticed that all of the waiters had strings hanging from their flies. My curiosity got the better of me and before he walked off, I asked the waiter, "Excuse me, but can you tell me why you have that string right there?"

"Oh, certainly!" he answered, lowering his voice. "Not everyone is as observant as you. That consulting firm I mentioned also found out that we can save time in the restroom."

"How so?"

"See," he continued, "by tying this string to the tip of you-know-what, we can pull it out over the urinal without touching it, and that way eliminate the need to wash hands, shortening the time spent in the restroom by 76.39 percent."

"Okay, that makes sense, but ... if the string helps you get it out, how do you put it back in?"

"Well," he whispered, lowering his voice even further, "I don't know about the others, but I use the spoon."

Bartainment training: Bartainment needs to focus on the entertainment and novelty of the concept.

Bartainer: This position is a difficult one to fill, often requiring dancing skills along with bartending skills in one employee. Training includes lots of dance rehearsals and rehearsing crowd interaction with microphones and props.

Dancer/entertainer: This position key entertainment-focused venues, with employees in concept-style uniforms, dancing and entertaining patrons.

Security: These employees will be busy looking after the safety of the female team members. I like bowling shirts on the security staff

Team Players

Training and promoting as a team up until opening is a good way to develop relationships and weed out any catty or problem employees. Develop your team members by teaching that teamwork and team spirit are more important than the individual.

Complaints

Dealing with complaints is always a case-by-case issue. When dealing with drunken and belligerent patrons, you must take many factors into account. The key to dealing with any situation is to diffuse it as quickly and quietly as possible.

When dealing with complaints, it is a good idea for the management team to handle the patron one-on-one, and with a security guard present if there is a threat of violence.

Complaints about team members or lack of professional standards should be dealt with immediately and honestly with a direct apology and an investigation and appraisal of the situation from upper management. Offering to buy a round of drinks for the patron and his guests is always a good idea to diffuse the situation.

Complaints about the venue's shortcomings can be dealt with differently from other complaints as they are often about the lack of bathrooms or the lack of seating. These are not immediately correctable, and your management team and team members should be aware of these issues already and have a prepared response, such as, "I apologize and we are currently working on correcting this problem in the near future."

Complaints from patrons about other customers are a more serious situation and need to be handled with great tact, quickly defusing and resolving the situation. These situations need to be dealt with fast before they escalate into violent altercations inside or outside your venue.

Common situations:
- A drunken patron harassing a female customer;
- A sober patron harassing a female customer;
- A drunken patron being overly loud and obnoxious;
- A patron can't walk straight and is colliding with other customers;
- A patron spills another customer's drink;
- Patrons having a dispute;
- Patrons have a dispute over someone of the opposite sex;
- A patron developing a case of liquid courage.

Most of these situations need immediate attention, and most likely, security team members will already be aware of these patrons' unsavory behavior and should be working to contain or remove them from the public area to a safe zone.

In the case of patron harassment, the security team should tell the offender that he will be removed if there is another complaint.

Any complaints involving direct contact with a patron who is drunk should be approached with tact and speed, immediately removing the drunken customer from the public area to a safe zone.

When diffusing these situations, follow these guidelines:
1. Establish safe zones in your venue. Safe zones should be away from any area that has public access. Depending on your venue's size, you may have numerous safe zones.
2. Immediately remove any drunken patron from public areas to a safe zone.
3. The removal process should be controlled and practiced. For example: security team member: "Hello, can I talk to you over here for a second, sir?" Then they quickly lead the patron to the safe zone.

The Capture
By shaking hands, holding on, then putting an arm around the patron's shoulders while you lead them away will let you quickly take control of the situation so you can easily lead them away to a safe zone.

4. Removing drunken patrons from public areas removes the customer's need to act out or show off in front of his friends or other people.
5. Immediately offer a cold bottle of water to the drunken patron when you arrive at the designated safe zone.

Psychology
Let the patron know you are only trying to help him and you are concerned about his well being."

6. Do not throw drunks out as quickly as possible. This is your patron and you are responsible for his condition and any immediate decisions he might make.
7. Hold this patron in the safe zone until you can find a friend or contact a taxi to take him home.
8. Always make a report of the incident, including his contact information, and make a photocopy of his ID.
9. Always pay for the taxi ride home if the patron does not have the money.

Being safe rather than sorry is going to make the overall environment and operation of your bar or nightclub for you, your insurance company and the local authorities much healthier.

As for patrons who have been affected by drunken customers, offer to buy them a drink and apologize for any inconvenience, informing them that the situation has been taken care of.

All complaints handled by the management team and team members should be discussed in the next employee meeting, and ways to resolve any shortcomings in the response and handling of the situation should be reviewed.

Having a team that is well informed and up to date on issues, with the training to handle problems as they arise, is the responsibility of the management team and ownership.

Meetings should be followed up with a short newsletter handed out with the paychecks. This is a good way of keeping the entire team in the loop as to any policy changes. How your team handles situations that arise from complaints reflects on the professionalism of your bar or nightclub. Patrons will recognize a professionally run operation.

Occupational Health & Safety Issues

A bar is a high-risk area. There are countless hazards to your team members. An injury to an employee or customer can result in a large insurance claim and the loss of a good and skilled employee, or worse.

Your security team will be the most likely candidates for serious harm or injuries. Other team-related injuries will arise from slips and falls, or back injuries from carrying heavy items.

Taking precautions to identify and mitigate the risks associated with workplace injuries is the responsibility of your management team.

Some simple items needed to prevent injury and reduce accidents are:

1. Rubber floor mats behind the bar.
2. Lighting in the exit and egress areas.
3. Easy access to first-aid kits.
4. Easy-to-locate fire extinguishers
5. Emergency exit plans
6. Alcohol awareness classes

It is important to assess potentially hazardous situations, such as a fire or large-scale fight, the areas those hazards may occur in, and what action can be taken to reduce the potential risks.

Exit plans and quick team-member reactions to serious incidents will reduce the likelihood of serious injury to employees and patrons.

Organization

It is important to get all your back-of-house systems in place.

- Organized storage areas;
- Inventory control systems;
- Breakage/spill forms;
- Order forms;
- Weekly inventory levels;
- Delivery dates and weekly times set with vendors.

For most of these systems, you will need a competent management team in place to track and update all related items of inventory from the beginning

Items to be tracked closely:
- Liquor
- Beer
- Wine
- Glassware/plastic cups
- Mixers

You will have to implement manual systems in the liquor and alcohol beverage storage areas, checking in and out items on sign-out forms and then transferring them to an Excel spreadsheet for a computerized inventory database when possible.

Failing to do inventory is the same as burning hundred dollar bills.

THE CUSTOMER

Who are these people, anyway? They come and go. They get drunk and belligerent. They get in fights and don't tip. And, as operators, we have a love-hate relationship with them.

People need to escape many things and seek new things.

Escape list	Seek
1-life	1-girlfriend/boyfriend
2-stress	2-New friends
3-reality	3-Good times/fun
4-lonleines	4-sex

Identify the customer you want by getting into the scene and talking with the people who are going out and partying. What are they drinking? What do they like for entertainment? Can you fill the many needs of these customers? You need to first know what those needs are.

´ I don't understand?

Please get drunk in my bar and spend every last dollar you have on all of your friends and the hot chicks in the bar. But spill a drink on someone while you are weaving to the bathroom to make room for more of my product and you will get hauled out by two towering security guards faster than you can slur out "WHHAaat thhEEE F*&%"

I love to just people-watch. This is the most interesting form of entertainment in a bar. Watching guys get shot down hard by one girl after another—even the ugly ones! You wish you could record this and show it to him when he is sober.

"I love you but you are so misunderstood."

Most bar and nightclub operators misunderstand their customers.

Just like a good spouse, an operator should listen to patrons' needs and understand that they are only doing what you want them to do: buy alcohol and have fun.

Promoting social interaction in your bar or nightclub

The dance floor is one of the greatest devices for promoting social interaction since the invention of beer and alcohol. Looking back on your own childhood, you have been introduced to many institutionalized social interaction activities:

Prom;
Winter formal;
Home-coming;
All of the other informal school dances you can remember.

These activities were all based around music and a dance floor, with boys on one side and girls on the other, both sexes nervous and tentative but brought together in order to create relationships and promote social interaction.

With alcohol added in the mix, inhibitions are lowered and acceptable social behaviors begin to fluctuate. Some people reach out for social companionship. Some people are able to open up and explore more diverse possibilities in a mate or companion. Alcohol plays a large role in breaking down the barriers between the sexes. This is referred to as liquid courage.

Most male patrons are looking to hook up, while many female customers love the idea of letting their hair down, having a good time and dancing all night.

Let's look at different ways to promote social interaction in your concept, Here are some ideas:

- A dance floor with small raised platforms, creating safe zones for women to dance unmolested. This also allows for potential eye contact between women and men.
- Communal tables for random groups of patrons to attach to in close proximity. This will promote a sharing of space and provide communication opportunities.
- Communal seating areas with pods, benches, booths or couches. This lets customers get closer to other patrons.

The Little Black Bar Book

- Games and activities, such as quizzes, pool and darts. This will promote interaction, help create competitions and promote teamwork. You can institute contests with prizes, including free drinks, food or gift certificates.
- Theme parties are always a huge hit, and there are many ideas to choose from. Here are some examples that I have been involved with in the past: white party, black Party, toga party, pimp and ho ball, fire and ice, and candy land.<<describe these here or elsewhere>>
- Fashion shows by local designers have been a big hit, with lots of local participation from hair salons and retail outlets. This is a good way to introduce models and their peers to your venue. Fashion shows also give patrons a good opportunity to interact.

Instincts

- How do I make the hunter and hunted come together in the same hunting ground?
- What is it that this animal wants?
- What does this animal need?
- What is it that makes these animals flock to this spot?
- What do I understand about this animal that my competition does not?

Always Take Care of the Women!

Things to be cautious of in your concept are your ratio of men to women. This is important to monitor as the more you are known as the spot with all the women, the longer and more likely you are to be the hot-spot. The phrase I have always used is: *Women like to look at women, and men like to look at women.*

If you stick to this philosophy, you will put your concept on top of others that seem to forget this.
1. Always cater to all women.
2. Always line pass women. Never make them wait in long lines.
3. Always make sure your door hosts acknowledge key female patrons quickly.
4. Make sure you protect the women from drunks.
5. Provide seating for the key female patrons who are your regulars, remember their names, and keep spots open for them every weekend.
6. Treat them like queens and they will return.
7. Listen to their needs and complaints, always keeping an open mind since need them, and when the next new bar or nightclub opens, they might not need you.
8. Make sure you have clean bathrooms with stocked paper wares and a full-length mirror.
9. Make sure you have enough women's toilets. The long lines are the worst.

Who Needs the Love? Women!

The easy answer is everyone, but the truth 90 percent of the time is women! If I had my choice, I'd want my patrons to be 70 percent women and 30 percent men, but this is not to be unless you open a lesbian bar. (I would like to say that I love lesbians!)

Most of your patrons will be men who are much more willing to put up with discomfort and other bullshit. A woman, on the other hand, is not about to deal with the hassles and shortcomings of a badly designed and operated venue.

How to Show Women the Love

- Show them the love with hugs, name recognition, European kisses, clean bathrooms, good service and soft toilet paper, and more toilet paper when those rolls run out.
- Seating is a good place to start. My feet hurt after standing around for eight hours in sneakers. How do you think women feel standing around in 4-inch-high stiletto heels?
- Safe dancing areas for women in any bar or nightclub is a good idea. With an area designated for female patrons to show off how hours in a salon and a new $300 dress have transformed them into beautiful, sexy, under-appreciated butterflies.

The Little Black Bar Book

- Please don't forget that men don't carry handbags. Designers don't ever think about where handbags or purses are supposed to go while taking a leak or dancing in front of a 1,000 drunken revelers. A simple hook that costs no more that 50 cents can get you hundreds of thanks. Hooks under tables, in bathrooms and at the bar are all perfect ,and all will find their moments of use.
- Something as simple as a small sticker placed on the back of their local ID will act as their VIP card, not take up any room in their wallet and never be forgotten.
- Convenience is easy to imagine, but since I am not female, I will truly never know. Do not be afraid to ask for suggestions from your female team members about what is needed to make your operation more female friendly.

Most operators will open the doors and be so busy with day-to-day and nighttime operations, they forget that making time to assess the needs of female patrons is overlooked until it is a problem. This is too late and problems should be identified and resolved before they become problems.

Rewarding good customers

The key question you should ask about your customer relations is: "How can I build a strong base of loyal customers?" Loyal customers will keep coming back over and over again. They are a powerful promotional force, with direct and influential access to both friends and peers.

What is a regular/VIP?

A regular is that familiar face you see every week in your venue. He or she comes in to have a good time, enjoying your place alone or with friends.

They often display patterns of behavior, such as having a favorite place to sit or ordering the same food or drink every visit. Once you have identified that regular, your team members should have already established a relationship with this patron. Establishing good communication between you and your team members will let you identify these patrons quickly and single them out for the special treatment they deserve.

These customers are often the backbone of the nightclub scene in most cities. A small group of patrons become the leaders of the party scene. These people should be identified and rewarded for their patronage. This group will be out almost every night of the week and have an established network of peers.

How do I reward the Regular or VIP?

Often, the smallest act can be reward enough for the regular. Let's look at some options.

1. Just saving the regulars a seating area for them can be one of the biggest things you can do. At a pub or a bar, you can have a small plaque put on the patron's bar stool.
2. In a nightclub, you can have a booth or seating area roped off for that regular who arrives every week for his or her table service. Nice little amenities can be added for this guest's convenience based on his regular needs: a curtain for more privacy, a small refrigerator, a phone installed to call from the booth directly to the bar, or a light switch turning on a light over the booth requesting service. This regular patron has high check averages and may have peculiar needs.
3. Customer mugs or engraved cups are always a great idea.
4. VIP cards are an easy and inexpensive reward, allowing for free entrance and passing the line.
5. Your regulars should be able to have guests with similar line privileges.
6. Separate entrance exceptions. This is for the larger nightclubs with numerous entrances. Allowing your regular to enter through a rear or side entrance is a true privilege
7. Comp taps can be used by your management team and team members to reward these regulars or VIPs.

MARKETING AND PROMOTIONS

Now that you know who your customers are, it is time to focus on how to market and sell your bar to the public. There are all the little things, such as business cards and flyers, to consider, plus the bigger questions of the best way to get access to your target market and let them know how great you are. The options are endless, but don't lose focus. Remember, your main attention should be on your target customers.

Finding a promotions team

Understanding market dynamics is important, and with the sudden growth of bars and nightclubs, you must be ready to identify existing and up-and-coming local talent in promotion niches, then integrate them into your marketing system. As a bar or nightclub operator or owner, you must be aware of what is happening around you in your local marketplace.

New and highly motivated promotions talent is always popping up. Most operators choose to ignore them or brush them off instead of nurturing them into a positive instrument for their bar or nightclub. If you encounter an up-and-coming promoter, don't be afraid to take a chance with one of your off nights. Remember, you have tools that can and will help him succeed.

Use your liquor representatives to help cover the costs of promotional materials. Allow the promoter to cross-promote on your other nights and work out a drink comp tab to let him interact and entice his guests and yours into attending the new event.

Your Marketing Plan Should Include:

Initial introductions into the market after the lease is signed

- A press release to the local media with a general, broad vision of the concept;
- An ad in the newspaper that reads: "New Bar/nightclub concept now hiring all positions";
- Ads, posters and banners on the outside of the venue. I would recommend a video projector running a short loop on a street-facing window.

Second Phase of the Marketing Plan During the Build-Out or Remodel

- During the hiring process, you will have the opportunity to promote to everyone who applies and start a great e-mail contact list for e-mail promotions.
- Write a thank-you letter to each and every one of the applicants and send them an invitation to your grand opening or one of the pre-opening parties.
- Now is the time to utilize the local media and set up interviews with the local magazines and newspapers. Developing a good relationship with these writers is always a good idea.
- If your budget is able to handle radio spots, find a local radio station with your demographics as their audience to hype your opening.
- TV coverage for the pre-opening or grand opening is always a huge bump. This will be played on your evening newscasts and is a nice push to patrons who would never have heard of or been aware of your concept without this type advertisement.
- Team members need to be instructed to promote to all of their friends, peers and patrons at their present jobs.
- Team member training will be followed by local outings to other bars and nightclubs in the area promoting your new concept with the new team members in uniform, logo hats and logo shirts.

Third Phase of the Marketing Pre-Opening Parties

1. First, you will do a "friends and family" party a week out from your public opening. Friends and family are just that: close friends and family members of the team. This should be limited to no more than 100 guests, and the purpose is to get real critiques on your entire operation.

You should have samples of your food constantly being delivered, testing your kitchen and staff's delivery process.

You should have your staff operating at full capacity and testing all of your systems, pushing to see what type of service quality you can deliver.

You will be testing all of your equipment: lighting, sound, video, POS system, bar, coolers, ice machine, kitchen, bathrooms and HVAC.

You will be finding the comfortable settings for the lighting and sound systems. You can adjust and mark the levels as the bar or nightclub gets busy, as ambient volumes rise and the sun sets.

You must have comment cards for every guest, with pens spread around for the guests to use.

These comment cards are important. I, for one, am deaf from years in the bar and nightclub business and can barely understand most conversations in a loud bar or nightclub. At the end of the night, sit down with your entire team and go over all of the comments.

Your friends and family are the people who will be forgiving and tell you the truth about issues that people drinking for free at your VIP party will not. This gives you a chance to screw up and have equipment screw up and your family and friends will be far more understanding and patient with these short-comings.

Allowing one day between your friends and family party and your first VIP party. This will allow for a correction of equipment failure and team member retraining. The most critical issue you will find will be your POS system. This usually needs the most attention and assistance through the entire opening process.

The construction company should be scheduled in the next morning at 6 a.m. to resolve any issues. This includes the plumber, electrician and carpenters.

2. The next party should be the press, media and local service-industry professionals VIP party. This event should include other owners and managers from other bars, nightclubs, restaurants, radio stations, newspapers, TV stations and other local promotional talent. This is where your team members and concept shine for your first real public audience. If you have a kitchen, you should deliver good-sized portions of your menu, from appetizers to entrées for your guests to sample. If you have specialty drinks, you should have your bar staff creating samples for your guests. Your team members should be able to handle this party easily and professionally, providing immaculate service.

3. The service-industry night VIP party is the big opening to the general public and should last no more than three to four hours of free drinks to all of the local service-industry workers. Every bartender, cocktail waitress, security guard, bar back, waiter, waitress and manager from every bar, nightclub and restaurant in the city should be invited.

Promotions for this event should start 30 days out from the event date and include business card-sized free passes to an open-bar bash pre-opening party. You should have your team members pass out between 5,000 to 10,000 invitations to all the service-industry employees in the area. You should arrange for your staff to move in teams throughout the city hitting, all of the bars, nightclubs and restaurants, passing out the invitations.

Marketing & Promotions

This is the time for the huge "Now Open" banner to be outside your venue.

4. Once you have ended the free service-industry VIP party, you should continue operating to the public, charging for drinks until your regular closing hours. Now, you will get ready for your grand opening party in about 30 to 45 days from your public opening. This will give you a big initial push and keep the hype going until your grand opening. Then you will get a second boost in revenue surrounding your grand opening weekend.

5. Your grand opening party should be aimed at your new regulars and the who's who of the party scene, including local models and celebrities. This is the time to establish your reputation as the place to be.
If you are a sports bar, you should invite local sports newscasters and local state or city teams down, including professional team members and coaches.

   If you are a live-music venue, you should have a big-name band or popular local band kick off this event for you, utilizing local talent and radio hosts.

6. The grand opening is the time to brand market your concept with free gifts of T-shirts and hats or other promotional logo items to your patrons. You also can include gift bags filled with items from local tanning salons, nail salons, restaurants and fashion retailers who will sponsor the gift bags and get a good promotion value out of your opening, also.

<u>Brand Marketing</u>

You need to establish your brand or logo if you are a BOBS, or bad ass sports bar. You need to push that brand. Place your branding on everything you can and in every way possible: hats, T-shirts, key chains, beanies, G-strings, poker chips, cups and beer mugs. Brand everything.

Your branded marketing must push and reinforce the branding of the concept, the name of your concept, and its location and hours of operation. When people think of sports, they will think of Bob's bar!

Continued Promotions

Once you are operational, the need for constant promotions is a must. You can utilize many different forms of promotions, from radio to local promotions teams to in-house promotions. It is important to know when a promotion is or is not working. You can figure out the success of a promotion by calculating your ROI. It should be no less than 50 percent. If you spend $2,000 promoting a big event and can generate over $4,000 in sales from that event, you have succeeded.

Some promotions, such as developing an off-night into a happening weekly event, could take one to two months of hard work and investment. You need to be the judge of when to cut your losses on a long-term promotional project.

You will find that some promotions fail because of your lack of understanding human habits. You must create habits, and habits do not happen overnight. They take time.

Often, bars or nightclubs will begin to develop a promotion based on a low drink special. This drink special is effective when it is targeted towards women, and often includes ladies drinking for free.

The owners, after a few weeks, are looking at a full house. "Wow, we are packed! Let's cut the special or adjust the special for the women. We don't need it anymore. We have a line outside the building and around the corner. Why should we continue to give away all our profits?"

"WRONG! This is a huge mistake made by most operators."

It takes time to develop a habit. Let's look at habits and habit-forming behavior. This promotion has been running for two months or 8 weeks. This promotion has only had eight real days of development. Out of those eight days, how many have your patrons made it to the venue? Maybe four.

This promotion might seem like it has been running forever to an operator who is in the bar every day, but to a patron, it just started.

This promotion should be run for six months to a year in order to create a functioning habit. You can raise profits different ways, such as increasing drink prices by a dollar to men or by adding a dollar or two to the men's cover charge to cover the cost of the liquor to the women. Don't pull the wheels off of the car before it dies!

"If it is not broken, don't try to fix it!"

Promotional Goal

Your goal is to create a profit-generating night out of a dark or slow night. If you were making $200 to $500 per night before the promotion and now your bar rings $5,000 to $6,000, with $2,500 to $3,500 in profit, this sound good to me. Just add in a small cover charge and you will have created a highly successful night. Let's say you were to charge a $2 to $5 dollar cover charge for men. If you are charging 80 percent of your male patrons, and you have 200 to 300 male patrons per night paying cover, you will increase your take by $400 to $1,500 per night. This is a big swing but every venue is different and has different parameters.

Spending Habits of Your Patrons?

This question is here because some bars and nightclubs base sales figures on check averages and figure, "Okay, if I had 1,000 guests and the bar did $10,000, my check average is $10 PPA, or "per person average" What is interesting is that some operators don't look deeper and research the true spending habits of their patrons.

Patrons' purchasing habits need to be tracked so you are not just ordering hundreds of cases of beer and liquor every week. Besides tracking sales on your POS system, you should actually hold an employee meeting on a Monday or pre-shift on a Thursday once a month and find out what type of transactions are occurring over the bar between patrons, bartenders and cocktails.

1-Do you have groups of patrons who consistently have large tabs and purchase high volumes of liquor? You then must figure out who these patrons are and target them for VIP attention.
2-Who is coming into your bar and taking up room by holding the same beer all night? These patrons need to be targeted in a category of harmless or not. If these are women, they are instantly grouped into the harmless category and always welcome.
3-Looking into different times of the month also makes a difference in patron-spending patterns, with weekends after paydays always showing higher sales totals than weekends in between.
4-A person, any person and all persons, are viable customers and they all will have their ups and downs, so be aware of who your regulars are and communicate with them. Reward their patronage with a round of drinks. I should be writing a book on the 15

cents to friendships, which is often what a cocktail costs you and the return in money. Loyalty, patronage and friendship are often priceless.

Does your target market have enough spare income to match your concept?

If you are looking at a college market, this is a good question to ask. If you are thinking about the high-end rock 'n' roll concept, you must be aware that $16 martinis are not going anywhere fast. But $3 dollar domestics are going to be golden bricks of liquid lying in your top loading coolers.

Sample Calendar for your Nightclub's First Year in Business

The big push to opening will be extremely stressful, requiring long hours and planning from your entire management team for a successful on-time opening. It is critical to have a promotional plan laid out.

Here is a sample calendar to help highlight some promotional strategies, along with a timeline of many of the time-critical elements related to pre-opening.

Let's set our calendar year opening date in early spring, as this will be the most opportune time to open any venue, and not New Year's, as many think. This will give you an entire spring, summer and fall of prime weather for your concept to develop.

After opening, you will need to begin developing your off-nights into profit-generating events. You can see how pre-planning and in-house promotions will be critical to the needs of your events.

Promotions and marketing includes radio, newspaper, flyers, outside promoters, street promotions teams and in-house promotions. These are all essential to the success of any promotional event that you are planning for your venue.

Be aware that developing new weekly and monthly events will take time and money, and you will need to invest lots of both if you want a good return. Finding sponsorship dollars for all of your events will be critical, as you will need assistance in financing the promotion costs. Your sponsors will assist you with money, product or creative compensation to help you get your promotional events off the ground and running.

Don't be afraid to cancel a promotional event if you believe that there is no way of it succeeding, or if it seems to be conflicting with other events.

Promotional strategies

1. Pre-opening parties;
2. Establishing sponsorships for events;
3. Establishing weekend nights
4. Establishing weekly events, such as SIN "Service Industry Night" and ladies nights;
5. Establishing monthly events, such as theme parties;
6. Establishing holiday events, such as Halloween and New Year's Eve

The Little Black Bar Book

JANUARY

SUNDAY	MONDAY	TUESDAY	WEDNESDAY	THURSDAY	FRIDAY	SATURDAY
	1 Set date for opening parties	2 Construction	3 Finish hiring management, construction	4 Begin promotions outings	5 Begin internet promotions	6 Promotions Construction
7	8 Begin liquor dist. Meetings.	9 Construction	10 Construction	11 Construction Promotions	12 Construction Promotions	13 Construction Promotions
14	15 Begin beer dist. meetings	16 Construction	17 Construction	18 Construction Promotions	19 Construction Promotions	20 Construction Promotions
21	22 Construction	23 Construction	24 Construction, Finish Hiring team	25 Construction Promotions	26 Construction Promotions	27 Construction Promotions
28	29 Construction	30 Construction	31 Construction Team orientation	Do you get the idea that promotions are very important?		

FEBUARY

SUNDAY	MONDAY	TUESDAY	WEDNESDAY	THURSDAY	FRIDAY	SATURDAY
				1 Training, Construction	2 Construction	3 Construction
4 Construction	5 Final Construction Health	6 Final Construction Plumbing	7 Final Construction Electrical	8 Final Construction Mechanical	9 Final Construction Fire Safety	10 Construction
11	12 Final Construction Call Backs	13 Aim for TCO or C of O here.	14 Add décor. Liquor licenses here!	15 Décor, a/v, begin dry goods delivery	16 Décor, A/V	17 Décor, A/V
18 Décor, A/V	19 Décor, Onsite training	20 Décor, Onsite training	21 Must have TCo, C of O & liquor licenses here!	22 Meeting, Décor, Stock Cleaning	23 Décor, Stock, Cleaning	24 Décor, Stock, Clean, alcohol
25 Meeting, stock, clean	26 Friends & Family Meeting	27 Afternoon Meeting	28 VIP night meeting	Make sure you have enough beer & liquor for the opening parties & a big weekend!		

Marketing & Promotions

MARCH

SUNDAY	MONDAY	TUESDAY	WEDNESDAY	THURSDAY	FRIDAY	SATURDAY
Sundays will be your SIN Service Industry Night beginning Sunday April 1st. You could hire an outside promoter.				1 Pre-Opening Party	2 OPEN	3 OPEN
4 CLOSED	5 Team Meeting Inventory	6 Construction needs	7 First Ladies Night	8 OPEN	9 OPEN	10 OPEN
11 CLOSED	12 Inventory	13 Construction needs	14 Ladies Night Begin Sunday Promotions	15 OPEN	16 OPEN	17 OPEN St. Patrick's Day
18 CLOSED	19 Inventory	20 Construction needs	21 Ladies Night	22 OPEN	23 OPEN	24 OPEN
25 CLOSED	26 Inventory	27 Construction needs	28 Ladies Night	29 OPEN	30 OPEN	31 OPEN

APRIL

SUNDAY	MONDAY	TUESDAY	WEDNESDAY	THURSDAY
1 First SIN opening party	2 Inventory	3 Monthly Cleaning & Repair	4 Begin May 5th theme party promotions.	5 Grand Opening Party!
				6 Grand Opening weekend blowot!
				7 Grand Opening weekend blowot!
8 SIN	9 Inventory	10	11 Ladies Night	12 OPEN
				13 OPEN
				14 OPEN
15 SIN	16 Inventory	17	18 Ladies Night	19 OPEN
				20 OPEN
				21 OPEN
22 SIN	23 Inventory	24	25 Ladies Night	26 OPEN
				27 OPEN
				28 OPEN
29 SIN	30 Inventory	31	Begin preparations for your first theme party on May 5th!	

The Little Black Bar Book

MAY

SUNDAY	MONDAY	TUESDAY	WEDNESDAY	THURSDAY	FRIDAY	SATURDAY
Next theme party Friday June 1st memorial Day weekend is the last weekend of the month.		1 Monthly Cleaning & Repair	2 Begin June 5th theme party promotions	3 Begin Thurs. specialty night promotions	4 OPEN	5 First big theme party
6 SIN	7 Inventory	8	9 Ladies Night	10 OPEN. Big Thurs. Coming Soon!	11 OPEN	12 OPEN
13 SIN	14 Inventory	15	16 Ladies Night	17 OPEN. Big Thurs. Coming Soon!	18 OPEN	19 OPEN
20 SIN	21 Inventory	22	23 Ladies Night	24 OPEN. Big Thurs. Coming Soon!	25 OPEN	26 OPEN Memorial Day Weekend!
27 SIN MDW!	28 Memorial Day!	29	30 Ladies Night	31 OPEN. Big Thurs. Coming Soon!	Begin Promotions for your Thursday Nights!	

JUNE

SUNDAY	MONDAY	TUESDAY	WEDNESDAY	THURSDAY	FRIDAY	SATURDAY
Big Thursdays night opens on the 7th. I would recommend having a cover band or live music or every BIG Thursday! Plan for your 4h of July bash them party RED, WHITE & BOOZE!					1 Theme Party	2 OPEN
3 SIN	4 Inventory	5 Monthly Cleaning & Repair	6 Ladies Night	7 Big Thursday!	8 OPEN	9 OPEN
10 SIN	11 Inventory	12	13 Ladies Night	14 Big Thursday!	15 OPEN	16 OPEN
17 SIN	18 Inventory	19	20 Ladies Night	21 Big Thursday!	22 OPEN	23 OPEN
24 SIN	25 Inventory	26	27 Ladies Night	28 Big Thursday!	29 OPEN	30 OPEN

Marketing & Promotions

JULY

SUNDAY	MONDAY	TUESDAY	WEDNESDAY	THURSDAY	FRIDAY	SATURDAY
1 SIN Promote Platinum	2 Inventory	3 Monthly Cleaning & Repair	4 Begin RED WHITE AND BOOZE! 4th of July	5 RED WHITE\ AND BOOZE	6 RED WHITE AND BOOZE	7 RED WHITE AND BOOZE
8 SIN Promote Platinum	9 Inventory	10	11 Ladies Night	12 BIG Thursdays	13 OPEN	14 OPEN
15 SIN Promote Platinum	16 Inventory	17	18 Ladies Night	19 BIG Thursdays	20 OPEN	21 OPEN
22 SIN Promote Platinum	23 Inventory	24	25 Ladies Night	26 BIG Thursdays	27 OPEN	28 OPEN
29 SIN Platinum Party	30 Inventory	31	Prepare for your month long beach party! Sand, Sun and Suds! You will decorate your venue for a month long beach party! Get sponsors Corona and Rum Brands! Staff wears swimwear!			

AUGUST 2007

SUNDAY	MONDAY	TUESDAY	WEDNESDAY	THURSDAY	FRIDAY	SATURDAY
Beach Party this month! Add decorations on the 1st! Add best bikini or swim suit cash prizes! Every night.			1 Ladies Night	2 BIG Thursdays	3 BIG BEACH PARTY	4 BIG BEACH PARTY
5 SIN TIKI PARTY	6 Inventory	7 Monthly Cleaning & Repair	8 Ladies Night	9 BIG Thursdays	10 BIG BEACH PARTY	11 BIG BEACH PARTY
12 SIN TIKI PARTY	13 Inventory	14	15 Ladies Night	16 BIG Thursdays	17 BIG BEACH PARTY	18 BIG BEACH PARTY
19 SIN TIKI PARTY	20 Inventory	21	22 Ladies Night	23 BIG Thursdays	24 BIG BEACH PARTY	25 BIG BEACH PARTY
26 SIN TIKI PARTY	27 Inventory	28	29 Ladies Night	30 BIG Thursdays	31 BIG BEACH PARTY	

The Little Black Bar Book

SEPTEMBER 2007

SUNDAY	MONDAY	TUESDAY	WEDNESDAY	THURSDAY	FRIDAY	SATURDAY
Clean the mess from your beach party! Get ready for another theme party "The White Party" September 30th					1 OPEN	
2 SIN Promote White Party	3 Inventory	4 Monthly Cleaning & Repair	5 Ladies Night	6 BIG Thursdays	7 OPEN	8 OPEN
9 SIN Promote White Party	10 Inventory	11	12 Ladies Night	13 BIG Thursdays	14 OPEN	15 OPEN
16 SIN Promote White Party	17 Inventory	18	19 Ladies Night	20 BIG Thursdays	21 OPEN	22 OPEN
23 SIN Promote White Party	24 Inventory	25	26 Ladies Night	27 BIG Thursdays	28 OPEN	29 OPEN
30 SIN White Party	Begin promotions for "The Black Party" on October 28th					

OCTOBER 2007

SUNDAY	MONDAY	TUESDAY	WEDNESDAY	THURSDAY	FRIDAY	SATURDAY
	1 Inventory	2 Monthly Cleaning & Repair	3 Ladies Night	4 BIG \ Thursdays	5 OPEN	6 OPEN
7 SIN Promote Black Party	8 Inventory	9	10 Ladies Night	11 BIG \ Thursdays	12 OPEN	13 OPEN
14 SIN Promote Black Party	15 Inventory	16	17 Ladies Night	18 BIG \ Thursdays	19 OPEN	20 OPEN
21 SIN Promote Black Party	22 Inventory	23	24 Ladies Night	25 BIG \ Thursdays	26 OPEN	27 OPEN
28 SIN Black Party	29 Halloween decorations	30 Halloween decorations	31 Halloween	Get ready Halloween weekend! Decorate the bar for Halloween, Employees in costume for the 4 nights! Use the décor from the Black Party!		

Marketing & Promotions

NOVEMBER 2007

SUNDAY	MONDAY	TUESDAY	WEDNESDAY	THURSDAY	FRIDAY	SATURDAY
You should have a costume contest for the patrons and one for the staff with prizes! Get ready for your SIN theme night RED!				1 BIG Thursdays Halloween	2 OPEN Halloween Party	3 OPEN Halloween Party
4 SIN Promote Red Party	5 Inventory	6 Monthly Cleaning & Repair	7 Ladies Night	8 BIG\ Thursdays	9 OPEN	10 OPEN
11 SIN Promote Red Party	12 Inventory	13	14 Ladies Night	15 BIG\ Thursdays	16 OPEN	17 OPEN
18 SIN Promote Red Party	19 Inventory	20	21 Ladies Night	22 BIG\ Thursdays	23 OPEN	24 OPEN
25 SIN Red Party	26 Inventory	27	28 Ladies Night	29 BIG\ Thursdays	30 OPEN	

DECEMBER 2007

SUNDAY	MONDAY	TUESDAY	WEDNESDAY	THURSDAY	FRIDAY	SATURDAY
You will have New Years and Christmas! Your SIN theme party will be GOLD for the New Years!						1 OPEN
2 SIN Promote Gold Party	3 Inventory	4 Monthly Cleaning & Repair	5 Ladies Night	6 BIG\ Thursdays	7 OPEN	8 OPEN
9 SIN Promote Gold Party	10 Inventory	11	12 Ladies Night	13 BIG\ Thursdays	14 OPEN	15 OPEN
16 SIN Promote Gold Party	17 Inventory	18	19 Ladies Night	20 BIG\ Thursdays	21 OPEN	22 OPEN
23 SIN Promote Gold Party	24 Inventory	25	26 Ladies Night	27 BIG\ Thursdays	28 OPEN	29 OPEN
30 SIN Gold Party	31 HAPPY NEW YEARS	What a great year now let's get ready for our big 1 YEAR ANNIVERSARY PARTY! The next SIN theme party will be up to you!				

Pricing Strategy

Your concept's pricing will be determined by the local marketplace. Look at similar concepts in the area and price accordingly. If your competition is charging $3 for domestic beer, don't think you can charge $5 or $6 for the same item. You must be sensitive to what your customer base is comfortable with.

Let's say you have just opened your bar and are packed and running strong. You are the first concept of your type in the area and are confident you can raise your prices. Be careful before you take this step; other types of businesses only can raise prices slightly. In the bar business, it is done in dollars, not cents. You cannot charge $2.75 for a beer as the nightmare of dealing with change will make your team members, accountant and management team want to jump off of the roof. Always charge in full dollar prices, even with low-volume bars or lounges. Just round up or down to the next full dollar amount.

When deciding to increase your prices, realize that you are not going to sneak this by your customers. They will notice, and if you raise it too much, you will find it will have an adverse effect on business. Maybe not at first, but down the line your customers may make decisions based on value. You don't want to be known as " that place with the $16 vodka Red Bulls," and by customers who don't even drink vodka Red Bulls.

You must be aware that even small price hikes need to be taken into consideration with local market conditions and competition.

1. Do other bars in the area have long lines?
2. Are other bars as busy as yours on the same nights?
3. Will your patrons notice a one dollar price increase?
4. Are you offering something such as a band or other entertainment that would warrant the raise?
5. Can you get higher profits without raising prices by highlighting other products such as draught beer?
6. Work with your distributors to get lower case prices or do an exclusive deal with a liquor vendor such as Skyy, Smirnoff or another vodka brand.

Marketing & Promotions

Price Wars

Some markets will go though phases when some bars and nightclubs will offer super-discounted drinks to patrons. This is done most often by failing concepts and bad operators.

What do you do in this situation?
- If they are offering 1 cent drinks till 9 or 10 p.m., this will have little affect on your concept as they are attempting to add filler patrons, which is just getting bodies into the venue during the early hours. This is a common tactic with large nightclubs.
- A bar offering free drinks for ladies all night. This is a great promotion with a strong drawing power. You must ask why the other bar is running this promotion. If a concept is failing, this is a strong play to make. A promotion such as this should run for the concept's remaining life. Most operations will run this promotion on an off-night, trying to develop this night. They will run it for awhile, then drop it once they feel they have a solid, steady crowd.
You must take quick action if you feel this is directly affecting you and is from a strong local competitor. Matching this promotion is the move to make but never go lower; that is the move you will leave to them. The only move for them is to give away the bar and only charge a cover to compensate. If they decide to give away the bar, just hold out but don't follow suit. Focus on what you are good at and hold steady while the other concept folds.
- I recommend having some form of communication with local bar and nightclub owners and operators. You can have lunch once a month with them and just talk about viable options for the area, including pricing strategies and promotional ideas. Don't forget that the synergy of all the local concepts is a positive force to attract more patrons to the area.

- Some bar and nightclub owners are just plain idiots and will only think of you as competition. In this case, you have no choice but to focus on your concept and market and keep an eye on what the other competitor is doing. You should still try to create lines of communication with other venues in the area. Alienating your business is never a good idea. Some good ways to create relationships is to invite the operators to your establishment and take care of them as you would want to be taken care of at their venues.
Offer them free tabs and preferential treatment for their guests who they send to you.
- Remember that the variables in every market and situation are different and you should think through other options before starting a pricing war.
- No one ever wins in a pricing war; there are only losers. Sure, the customers save some money but soon they will have fewer options as bars and nightclubs shut down, leaving fewer venues with fewer options for customers. The remaining bars and nightclubs will now have longer lines and be more crowded than ever while new concepts start up again to take the place of the fallen businesses

STEP BY STEP QUICK REFERENCE GUIDE

Here are some of the steps involved in opening a new bar or nightclub:

- Researching the local market;
- Designing the concept;
- Writing a business plan for investors;
- Establish finances and using "creative fundraising;"
- Finding a location and lease negotiations;
- Selecting a contractor, architect, interior designer and bar consultant ;
- Designing the concept to fit the location or the location to fit the concept;
- Finding a lawyer for the liquor, beer and gaming licensing;
- Finding a CPA firm or accountant;
- Submitting your plans and designs to the city;
- Construction and décor;
- Hiring of management and staff;
- Sourcing suppliers and preparing initial orders;
- Promotional push, marketing campaign and press releases;
- Final inspections and license approvals in place;
- Training and educating staff;
- Operational systems;
- Soft opening;
- Grand opening 30 days later;

A Few Critical Path Items and Key Points

The standard operating procedures of a bar or nightclub are critical elements. They begin with the principal members setting the standards by hiring a good management team. With this team, you will develop the operating procedures from experienced bar operators.

Once you have your management team in place, along with an idea of the concept, you will be able to move forward with the development.

- The design and construction of your venue are important as to how efficiently your staff will be able to work and generate revenue.

- It is a good idea for inexperienced bar or nightclub principals to have a bar consultant, architect or interior designer contributing to the initial planning stages of your venue.

- Recruit an experienced management team.

- The development and implementation of solid operational procedures will determine your level of preparedness.

- Set the level of service standards for your venue. Design the training manuals and a training program that will ensure you achieve the quality of service you desire.

- Hire a team and train that team within the guidelines of your concept.

- Ordering stock and supplies, setting inventory levels for that stock, setting up your point-of-sale ("POS") system, setting up your theft prevention and video surveillance systems.

Timing Does Matter

Timing plays an important role. You don't want to open in the middle of a Chicago winter when you will have to deal with extreme weather.

You want to be aware of other bars or nightclubs opening around the same time period (within 60 days) as the honeymoon period will be in full swing for the other concept. If this seems like it will occur, you must look at the other concept's opening and how far it is from your location. Will this other concept be targeting your demographic? In a larger market, this will have less of an impact on both concepts.

A Quick Overview of the Steps to Opening a Bar or Nightclub

Opening a bar is a major undertaking and will require a huge investment of time from the key principals involved. The following steps are laid out to give those principals some insight into what tasks actually need to be performed and what order they will need to occur in.

Every venue will have different sets of obstacles and challenges, and how long and complicated those obstacles are will differ with every venue.

Responsibilities List

This is an overview of items that need to be performed for your operation to move forward. Below is an abridged version of a project checklist:

- The task;
- The task or item details;
- The task or item and the responsibilities for the principal members;
- The timeline (an estimation of time needed for each task to be executed);
- Financial requirements, such as deposits or other needs for the different phases

PROJECT STARTS HERE

Business Plan

It is a good idea to have a plan on paper for any project. The initial business plan should cover many aspects of your bar or nightclub opening. You should include your concept description, your mission statement, how much you believe the total cost for the project will be, and a three-year profit-and-loss statement. You might require advice or assistance to finish your business plan, and any of these experienced professionals can assist you: an attorney, accountant, CPA, architect, interior designer, bar or nightclub manager, and a bar consultant.

Responsibility: Principals, experienced help
Timeline: 1 week

Conduct Research on the Local Competition

Now is the time for you to do some intense market research. You must get out and hit the pavement, seeking out potential gaps or shortcomings in the marketplace.

It is important to identify the need for a particular concept or a better version of an existing concept in your marketplace. If you have a specific concept in mind, search out other similar concepts and research them to discover what they are doing right or wrong. Then, begin searching for an area to locate your concept away from similar concepts.

Responsibility: Principals
Timeline: 1 week to 1 month

Create a Budget

In order to create an accurate budget, you will need data from your contractor, information about your lease and location,, proposed décor ideas, initial liquor orders, dry-goods needs, legal fees, licensing fees and costs, labor and payroll estimates, and management salaries.

Many pieces of information are going to be required to formulate a budget. Using an Excel spreadsheet can help to make this task easier.

Inputting this information into the spreadsheet will give you an idea of the total funds needed to get the project off the ground. It also will tabulate the costs of supporting the project for its first three to six months.
Responsibility: Principals and a bar or nightclub management professional
Timeline: 1 week - 1 month

Create a Business Plan for Raising Capital

If you have no experience in the bar and nightclub business, you should enlist some professionals to give you a hand with the business plan's financial sections.

You will need an introduction naming the principals involved and their experience in the business or any other roles they will play. You will need an accurate description of your concept and ideas. You also will need a three-year P&L spreadsheet showing investors their potential returns.

You will need a financial statement from each of the principals involved in the project.

You will need a spreadsheet detailing the total estimated cost of the project and the total capital needed. You will need a timeline outlining the different phases of the project.

You can find sample business plans on the Internet or at an Office Depot or other business supply store.
You will need to seek out possible investors, banks, sponsors, alternative lending institutions such as "Advance Me." Your last alternative would be an SBA loan.
Responsibility: Principals and a bar or nightclub management professional
Timeline: 1 week - 1 month

Submitting Business Plans to Possible Investors or Your Bank

Submitting your business plan to potential investors and banks to secure the financing to build your bar or nightclub will be difficult at best. Finding investors is a hit-or-miss proposition. You will need to start finding local investment groups such as a group of doctors, attorneys and real-estate brokers. This is a group of investors who are willing to take higher risks, have large taxable incomes and often need write-offs.

Offering incentives to any individual for finding investors is a good way of spreading the word. Use all of your contacts and personal relationships to find and locate possible investors.
Banks will rarely give you a loan. You have a better chance of getting a personal line of credit.
Responsibility: Principals
Timeline: 1 day – 2 month

Quick Step Reference Guide

Looking for a Potential Site

You are going to need to find a potential venue. Keep in mind that location, accessibility and parking are extremely important factors.

The three magic rules to follow in finding a venue are: LOCATION, LOCATION, and LOCATION!

Usually, paying a higher lease and having an established location with a high-volume of traffic is a less risky proposition than paying a third of the price but being off the beaten path.

This is a business of risk and reward and having a firm understanding and knowledge in your marketplace will help you to realize what is possible. If you can wait for the best location, wait. If it is meant to be, it will be.

Keep in mind that lease negotiations take time and never rush into a lease. Always keep your options open and look for alternative venues to use as backups.
Responsibility: Principals
Timeline: One day to forever.

Finding an Attorney

You may need multiple attorneys for the project's different aspects: state business licenses, local business licenses, liquor licenses, beer Licenses, operating agreements, contract reviews and sometimes lease negotiations.

Attorney's fees can run into the tens of thousands of dollars. Once you have a location, you will need an attorney to begin processing your liquor and beer licenses. This will take a considerable amount of time in some cities.

Make sure your attorney has experience in similar types of concepts in the same city or district.
Responsibility: Principals and attorneys
Timeline: 2 Days

Deciding on a Venue

Once you have found a possible venue or venues, you must make arrangements to enter and inspect it. Does it fit your needs? Is it the correct size? Was it a bar or restaurant before and is it equipped? Does it have enough secured parking and is the location suitable to your client base?

Having a broker assist you may sometimes help and sometimes hurt as broker fees can be huge. Unless the broker can negotiate a below-market price with the landlord, he or she will only cost you and the landlord more money.

Take plenty of pictures and videotape of the entire venue on your first walk-through. This will cover you for future liabilities.

If you believe the venue you have selected has possibilities, you will want to place a deposit, locking it up and allowing you time to negotiate with the landlord.
Responsibility: Broker and Principals
Timeline: 1 week to 1 month
Financial: Deposit

Lease Agreement

Once you have found a possible venue, you must begin your lease negotiations. This is an extremely difficult and potentially disastrous time for many bars.

"YOU CAN DESTROY YOUR ENTIRE DREAM HERE AND NOW."

Rule No. 1: TAKE YOUR TIME! Too many times, I have seen owners destroy any chances they have of making a successful and profitable concept by rushing into a bad lease. They will overpay on the square footage or not receive any tenant-improvement dollars from the landlord. This is the largest, single, monthly expense you will ever have.

Get an attorney involved or a bar and nightclub professional. The landlord would like nothing better than to have you spend hundreds of thousands of dollars upgrading his venue, locking you into a binding lease, and seeing you fail, leaving him with expensive improvements added to his building at no cost to him.

Do some research. Find out what the landlord paid for the building and what the going square-foot market price is for the venue and other venues in the same area.

Are there any city or state zoning restrictions for bars or nightclubs in the venue you have selected? You must have an escape clause in the lease in case the venue cannot be licensed for any reason.
Responsibility: Principals and your attorney
Timeline: 2 weeks to 3 months
Financing: Deposit required for the lease

Hiring Architects/Interior Designers/Bar Consultants

If you have never opened a bar or nightclub, it is a good idea to hire someone who has some previous experience. It will cost you in the short-term but save your ass in the long run.

You are going to require a team. After starting with an experienced principal or consultant, finding an architect/interior designer is the next step.

Warning: Architects and interior designers very often are not familiar with the needs of a bar or nightclub 90 percent of the time, and they often get their little feelings hurt when industry professionals try to help by offering key design ideas based on experience!

Since architects and designers had to go to school for a long time to learn that fuchsia is a color and that earth tones look fabulous with oranges and dark woods, we wouldn't want to get into a slap fight this early into the project.

Just because someone has designed a restaurant that cost over $400 per square foot only means that this person has no idea of the wear and tear put on a happening bar or nightclub, and the pictures they show you in their portfolio may not match the condition of that bar or club after six month of heavy use and traffic. People don't understand the amount of maintenance and money needed to keep it looking that good.

Design it to last! Design it to work! Design it to function!

Responsibility: Principals
Timeline: 1-2 weeks
Financing: Deposits needed for the specialists

Designing Your Concept

Many bar owners with whom I have worked think that because they go to bars all the time, they somehow know how to build a bar. I have heard stupid statements like, "I want my bar to be just like that bar!" They will then try to copy that other bar. Why not just hire the designer of that other bar, you moron?! I'm sure that he or she has other equally great design ideas!

It is important that your design works with your venue's concept. Having some knowledge of city codes and regulations—along with a working knowledge of bar equipment, placement, design and basic finishing materials—is critical to keeping your budget and timeline in order.

The interior designer and architect can both design and create your concept for you. They must be kept on a short leash as they will give you the mother of all bars but charge you for designing a dream you cannot afford to build. They need to understand your budget and stick to it.

Bar consultants can sometimes be a pain in the ass. They have a good understanding of what works and what doesn't. This occasionally makes them tough to work with, as they get frustrated with the owners', designer's and architect's hair-brained ideas and not having their suggestions and advice heeded.

"No One Wants Their Name on a Failed Project"

This can be best summed up by the Fed-EX commercials that have the guy working with all the monkeys!

You must have a licensed architect for your project, and the architect will handle all of the drawings that need to be submitted to the contractors for bidding and the city for permits.

An interior designer will handle the finishes, decorative structures, furniture, fixtures and all of the finished materials needed for the venue.

The bar consultant hangs out and gets overpaid to tell you what to do while you don't listen to him. In the meantime, your bar or nightclub goes over budget and eventually fails! Of course it is entirely the consultants' fault.
Responsibility: Principals, architect, Interior designer and Bar Consultant
Timeline: 1 Month

Speaking to Contractors

This motley group of construction professionals will be the builders of your bar. They will handle all issues related to the construction and planning between your venue, the city and landlord.

If you don't understand construction, these contractors can smell blood in the water like a shark. They will circle your bloated, floating carcass, tearing off chunks of meat at their leisure.

Sorry about that! You should remember that contractors are here to make money and finish your concept as quickly as possible … before moving on to the next carcass.

Contractors will have fees of usually up to 10 percent, depending on the size of the project. Contractors work with sub-contractors, or "subs," who sometimes kick back to the contractors on the other end of the project.

The fees for a contractor can run from 5 percent to 10 percent of the total job. So, if you are a $100,000 project, they will make $10,000 plus the kickback from their subs.

Not all contractors are dishonest, and most will treat you fairly. Have a good base knowledge of construction and track the work with a daily log or diary. Keep track of the work performed and how many construction people worked that day, along with how many hours they logged. Keep an eye out for overtime work. Keeping a log will come in handy as you begin paying out for the different construction phases being completed. Invoices for completed work can be cross-checked with your log.

You will need to get multiple copies of the blueprints from your architect and give them to every contractor to let them generate a bid for your project.

Picking the lowest bidder is not always the best choice. Just because we built the space shuttle that way doesn't mean it's the right way. Just look at the space shuttle's track record.

Look for a contractor with previous experience building bars and nightclubs and who understands the special needs for liquor-serving venues.

Look for a contractor who has a good working relationship with the city planning department and building inspectors.
Responsibility: Principals, Bar consultant
Timeline: 1-2 weeks

The Bid Process with Contractors
You must have the most complete set of plans outlining your project, with as much detail as possible about the construction needs. This is so you can get more exact bids from the contractors.

You should have a minimum of three different contractors bidding on your project. This will give you a median number to work with once all of the bids come in.

When the bids have been turned in, you need to compare them and figure out the discrepancies. For example, one bid might have electrical at $45,000 and another at $15,000. Someone is way off. You need to find out why these numbers are where they are.

Some contractors will low-ball the initial bid to get the job, and then hammer you with change orders and contract specifics that require costly additions and changes.

Once you have decided on a contractor, you must sign a standard American Institute of Architects (AIA) contract. This is a standard legal document used nationwide for contractors.

It is essential to establish a final design that includes input from an interior designer, architect and bar consultant.

One way for contractors to bid on a job is with a T&M (time and material) agreement. T&M means they are going to bill you based on the time and materials for the project, no matter what it takes to complete the job. They will end up milking the job, in this case.

Instead, choose a "Not To Exceed" bid. This means that if the contractor and his subs say it will cost $10,000 to get the electrical done and it ends up being $13,500, the contractor and his subs will cover the difference.
Responsibility: Principals, bar consultant
Timeline: 2 weeks
Financing: Deposit needed for the contractor

Licenses

You must start with your state business licenses, local business license, liquor license and beer license.

Don't forget to lock in the name of your business with the secretary of state. You will need to register the name under which you are doing business with the state. You also will need to search the state database and make sure that the name is not already in use.

Once you have the venue and the lease in place, your attorney must begin the application process for your liquor and beer licenses.

Some districts may require a live-music permit, dance hall permit and promoter's license. These can be obtained by the principals or handled by your attorney.

Liquor and beer license applications require a background check of the principals, who will need to include personal financial statements. Every principal investor over a certain percentage will be required by law to go through this process. The percentage varies from state to state.

All of these processes and licenses, including your attorney, will cost money and need deposits. You will need to have an account in which you can write checks in the name of the company or LLC as soon as possible.

You will need to meet with the local city council to get the necessary approvals to open your business. Your liquor attorney should arrange this for you. It is often easy and takes only a few minutes. You will present yourself to the city council and your attorney should outline your request to open a bar or nightclub at your selected location. The council will then decide if it is in the best interest of the city to permit such a business in that location. The council will then ask if there is anyone present who opposes the motion to allow you to operate your venue in that location.

Most every city or state will require a bond for your liquor and beer licenses.
Responsibility: Principals, Attorney
Timeline: 2-3 days for paperwork and up to 3 months for background checks

Opening a Bank Account and hiring a Payroll Company
You will need your business license in hand to open your bank accounts. Open two accounts: one for construction monies in the beginning and one for operations and payroll needs. This second account should have a limit on withdrawals and a check-amount maximum of $1,000.

The first account will switch over to be your deposit account for daily and weekly sales. This will be your main account and you will use the other account only for payroll.

The separate payroll account will be used by you for your payroll service provider: ADP, Intuit or another company.

You will need to fill out the account signature card with the selected principals as signatories on both accounts. Your general manager should be a check signer on the second limited account, also, with the ability to cut checks up to $1,000.

You will need to order a carbon-copy, ledger-sized checkbook.

Responsibility: Principals, general manager when hired
Timeline: 1 day

With the Finalized Drawings and Your Contractor Selection Complete
Now is the time to have your contractor or architect go to the city and submit your plans to the building department. You will need three full-set copies for the city building department. These need to be full sets and full size.

You will receive the demo plan quickly, if you haven't already, and be able to begin construction. It is possible to receive your demolition permit early by having your architect do a quick single-sheet blueprint for the city, outlining the areas for proposed

demolition. Your contractor can then submit the demo plan to the city, which, in most cases, can be stamped and approved over the counter the same day.
Responsibility: Principals, Attorneys
Timeline: 1 day

Landlord Prepares Building for Handover to You and Your Contractor

The landlord and you will concur in the lease agreement the condition in which the building is to be handed over to you.

Beware: Asbestos is common in older buildings. It can be found in the tiles, popcorn ceilings, vinyl floor tiles, even the glue used to hold the floor tiles down.

In your lease agreement, you will want the building delivered as close to what is known as a "vanilla shell." The vanilla shell condition is a bare-wall and bare-floor venue clean and clear of clutter and trash.

If it had hardwood flooring and you will be reusing the same flooring, you will want the flooring left in place. But if you will be tiling the floor, you will want the flooring removed by the landlord.

Your selected contractor will take over the building. If possible, you should set up your office in the venue with fax, Internet and phone lines. This will be your home away from home.
Responsibility: Principals, contractor.
Timeline: 1-2 days

Your Contractor Begins Work

Your demolition permit will be the first over-the-counter permit to be filed by your contractor. You can then begin the process of removing unwanted structures and preparing the venue for the first phase of construction.

The actual building permit may take anywhere from 30 days to 3 months to be approved by the different departments inside the building department.

In the meantime, you will be able to begin construction in the "rough in" phase. You must, however, leave everything open and exposed for the city inspectors before you can move on to the next phase of construction. This means that electrical conduits, plumbing pipes and chases—even walls—can be built but you cannot cover or hide these items and they must be visually inspected by the city inspector.

City departments you will need approval from are fire and life safety, health, plumbing, electrical and structural. If any of these departments find discrepancies in your drawings, your architect will need to correct the drawings and resubmit them to the city.

These are known as "red lines," and are marked on your drawings for your architect to identify and correct.
Responsibility: Contractor
Timeline: Laid out in a timeline to you by the contractor showing your date of completion

Signage

Your local sign company will handle the permit process and the design of your sign.

You must contact local sign companies for your exterior sign. This is an item that could take months to get approved and installed, as many cities have local historic commissions with strict zoning requirements regarding exterior signage.

If your district is very strict with signage, find out what company has installed other signs in the immediate area and contact them directly. They will have the most current information and working knowledge of what is required and allowed for your venue's signage.
Responsibility: Principals
Time: 2-3 days

Begin Your Advertising Campaign

Now is the time to begin your advertising campaign by placing posters or banners promoting your new venue in the windows announcing "Venue X Coming Soon Spring 2008!"

The city will want the widows covered during the construction phase, anyway, so why waste prime advertising space?

You will need to hire a graphic designer to create your logos and branding. This will be used on all of your advertising from here on out.

You must formulate your identity and project that out to the public, creating the hype for your venue.

Put together a small press release about your new venue and the principals involved. Contact local magazines, newspapers and local rags that have a local scene department and submit your press release. Ask to set up an interview with a reporter to do a story on the birth of your new venue.
Responsibility: Principals, graphic designer
Timeline: 1 week

Begin Hiring Management and Key Staff Members

When opening a new concept, you will have hundreds of tasks to perform that will never be repeated during daily operations. You will need help, and lots of it, as most of your systems must be built and designed from scratch. This will be a long, hard road, filled with detailed and mundane tasks that are all equally important in some way.

You will have to find the captain of this ship, if it is not going to be one of the principals. Finding a good general manager who understands the local scene and does not have a bad reputation may be difficult.

In some situations, you might find that you want to hire a competent assistant general manager from a local bar or nightclub and elevate them to be your general manager.

You might be lucky to be in a market where you will have a huge selection of very experienced operators with bar, nightclub or restaurant experience, and you will be able to choose from many talented candidates.

Interviewing for candidates for the key management positions is difficult, as all will have strengths and weaknesses.

Things to look for in a good general manager:
- Drive
- Dedication
- Stress management
- A variety of experience
- Leadership
- Charisma
- Local market experience

A good general manager, or GM, should be a good leader with the skills to oversee all operations, promotions, marketing, training and staffing. The GM also should be able to motivate all the team members under his or her supervision. The GM is not a bean-counter, and the tasks of accounting and bookkeeping should be left to experienced personnel.

"The best GMs are a jack of all trades!"

You may need a "key employee." This is someone who will need to pass a background check with the city the same way the owners and principals had to for the liquor license application. A key employee is a member of the management group who is recognized by the city, state and local officials as a main decision maker and operator who understands the laws and is responsible for the venue's safe operation.

Some states and cities require a key employee to be onsite at all times during operations.
Responsibility: Principals
Timeline: 1 week to 1 month

The Building Department and Your Contractor

During the construction phases, your contractor will deal directly with city inspectors who will perform multiple onsite inspections. The first is the rough-in phase. This is needed before you can finish walls or flooring. You will have to be signed off by the inspector for every trade or sub-contractor onsite for electrical, plumbing, HVAC and fire sprinklers, if needed. Next is the "testing phase," which is the final sign-off for each sub-contractor. This is needed before you get your final inspection from the main building inspector for your occupancy permit.

The ultimate goal is to receive your C of O (certificate of occupancy). If you are unable to get this, you can get a TCO, or Temporary Certificate of Occupancy, while you finish small details to satisfy the city building department.
Responsibility: Contractor, architect, principals
Timeline: Start of construction until finish.

Health Department

Handling the health department can be done by the principals or GM. The health department is very easy to locate using the local phone book. Once you find the office, take a quick trip down to visit or call to make an appointment with the local health inspector who will be handling your venue.

The health department people are extremely nice and always quite helpful. You will need to provide a few things to them. One will be your menu. You don't need to panic; just a simple MS Word document with a generalization of your menu is fine. They will need an equipment layout. This can be done on a Word file or drawn out. It is best to provide them with a copy of your blueprints with the equipment schedule and layout.

Remember, many cities and states have different regulations. Many districts will have different fee structures and will require you to fill out the needed forms, so don't forget to bring your checkbook.

Once you get all of your bar and kitchen equipment in place, you or your contractor can give them a call to inspect your venue. Don't panic when they hand you a list two-pages

long with items that need to be addressed. They will give you plenty of time to correct those issues.
Responsibility: Principals, GM
Timeline: 1 day

Meeting with Police and Local Alcohol and Beverage Control Authorities

It is important to establish good relations with the police and local authorities. You are a new concept and they will be patrolling and policing your area. The authorities will often be called when an incident involving patrons occurs, particularly when one party wishes to press charges. Having a good relationship and the support of the local authorities is important.

It is also important to get business cards and direct contact information for your emergency call list in your office from all of the local authorities.

- Police
- Fire
- Ambulance
- Liquor control

Be aware that you will have authorities visiting your establishment looking for liquor law violations, such as underage patrons. You will need to have solid systems in place safe-guarding yourself and your venue from your own team members' shortcomings. Your relationship with the local authorities is important as they can assist you in setting up systems that will help you enforce the law and protect your investment.
Responsibility: Principals, Management
Timeline: 1 day

Sourcing Management

It is important that you begin getting your management team in place. Depending on the size of your operation, you may need a broad range of managers or multiple managers in key positions.

- Assistant manager
- Bar manager
- Head of security

Your management team's final size will depend on the size of your venue and the total days and hours you will be open to the public.

Finding and hiring the backbone of your concept will be a challenge as you will find many talented candidates for these positions.

Look for:
- Management who have local bar and nightclub experience in other hot and popular concepts.
- Dedication and a commitment to long hours of work without complaining.
- Loyalty.
- Candidates who have a good following of employees and service staff from other bars and nightclubs.
- Managers who have developed strong relationships with the local customer base.

Responsibility: Principals, General Manager
Timeline: 1 week to 1 month

Setting Up Your Office

Once your management team is hired, you will need to outfit your office to accommodate all of your new staff. You will need to allocate space for your security camera system and your POS server.

Your staff will need a printer, phone lines, computers, a safe, wireless Internet access and standard office supplies and equipment. Also, having a document shredder is a good idea.

Don't forget your money counting machines!
Responsibility: Relevant management
Time: 2-3 days

Insurance

Finding affordable insurance in the bar and nightclub business is a joke and you must call around and get as many quotes as you can. *Don't forget to have the strike clause where you are covered for fights.*
Responsibility: Principals
Time: 1-2 weeks

Finding an Accountant and a Bookkeeper

You will need to find an accountant who is a licensed CPA. These are never cheap or easy to find.

Fill the bookkeeper position with an older, mature woman who will have no problem working the early daylight hours while your management team recovers from the previous night.

The bookkeeper should be on staff five days a week, Monday to Friday, and be on call Saturday and Sunday for a few hours. The bookkeeper's responsibilities will be to reconcile deposits, accounts payable, accounts receivable and payroll management. She should have a good working knowledge of QuickBooks, Excel and Microsoft Word.

A licensed CPA is needed to cover your butt from the IRS. Try to find a creative accountant with bar and nightclub experience (wink wink!)
Responsibility: Principals
Timeline: 1 week

Creating Standard Operation Procedures
Your management team should begin to create all of the operating procedures, such as schedules, inventory forms, spill forms, security incident reports, training manuals, food and drink menus, etc.

Responsibility: Management team
Timeline: 2-4 weeks

Finalizing the Legal Requirements and Planning for Your Opening
Make sure your licenses are moving forward and in line to be approved. This is very important to finalizing an opening date.

Your attorneys will have a good idea of the timeline for the approval of the liquor and beer licenses. You must work with this information and the contractor's timeline to coordinate your opening dates. I recommend adding a week to 10 days in order to compensate for missed deadlines and construction delays. This also will buy you time to install finishing touches.

Once you feel you have a solid date for opening, you will need to begin the marketing campaign push toward this date. You also will need to begin planning your opening parties.
Responsibility: Attorney, principals, contractor
Timeline: 2-4 weeks

Begin Sourcing Your Distributors and Suppliers
Now is the time for your management team to begin contacting all suppliers for the items your bar will need to operate.

Your management team will most likely be fielding dozens of distributors for every item imaginable in the bar business. You will have liquor, wine, beer, glassware, napkins, toilet sanitary products and everything else arrive in a wave of salesmen.

You must sift through all of these items and figure out what are useful and what distributors supply the products you need.

Your management team will be left with price lists from hundreds of liquor and wine brands, and they must figure out what will work with your concept, and what type of volume your concept can expect to sell on a weekly basis. That way, you can negotiate for price breaks based on volume.

Use plastic and not glass. Even for a nice lounge, except for Champagne or wine glasses, you can get plastic wares that look and feel very close to real glass, and the replacement factor and cost savings are huge over time.

If you have a bar or pub, cheap, plastic stacking cups are faster to use, cheaper and more efficient. These single-serving cups are safer than hard-plastic cups. They go right into the trash and don't shatter when dropped or thrown.
Responsibility: Management team
Timeline: 1 month

Sourcing Furniture and Other Bar Equipment
Your choices are to use secondhand equipment or order new equipment. Both are acceptable. If you are trying to save money, purchasing used equipment is a good way to go. Leasing is also a viable option, which will help ease your initial investment.

Furniture will be among the last items placed in your venue before you open. Finding good, durable, high-quality furniture for a bar or nightclub can be costly.

The Internet is the best place now to find vendors who make custom booths and banquets. You can order them in finished sections or have them designed to fit your space requirements. Furniture has a long lead time and will take weeks to build and ship to you.

First, search the local papers and Internet for places that are going out of business and purchase your equipment and furniture from them. It could be as cheap as 10 cents on the dollar. You can sometimes find the strangest things that end up being a perfect fit your bar or nightclub.

Used-equipment purveyors in most cities will remove equipment from closed-down bars, restaurants and nightclubs. They will repair and clean the equipment, and then sell it in their warehouses.

Remember, you can recover or repair any piece of furniture that is used or damaged..
Responsibility: Principals, Interior Designer, Management team
Timeline: 1-2 weeks

<u>Coke or Pepsi</u>
You will need to make a decision: Who will supply your bar guns and soda stations? Every marketplace has one dominant company. I prefer to use Pepsi as I find its service to be of high quality and its sometimes-free ice wells are attractive.

Contact your local rep and meet with him. You will get a credit application. Ask for national pricing. Tell them you are going to open another location soon in another city. That might be a lie, but it might work!

Once you have decided on whom to use, you need to schedule an installation date and coordinate with your contractor for when the bar will be ready.

You will need a close location for your bag in the box. Try to not to let piping run through an area such as the ceiling. It may get extremely hot during the summer months, and this will cause the soda to become flat. You will need power for the compressors at the bar and a water line with a back-flow preventer.
Responsibility: Bar Manager, Soda Company, Contractor
Timeline: 1 week

<u>Merchandise</u>
Find a supplier to handle all of your brand and logo wear items. These could include hats, T-shirts, tank tops, beanies, panties, jackets, etc. These also can be on your staff uniforms. For my opening parties, I like to give away about $5,000 in logo wear to girls. Hot chicks wearing tight tank tops with your logo on it are great advertisements!

You will need to have your logo on disc for the supplier. They will create a catalogue of their items with your logo on it.

This is a long lead item and needs to be ordered far enough in advance. Try to get sponsors to pay for your merchandise!
Responsibility: Management
Timeline: 2-3 days

Sound and Lighting

Hire a local, professional audio-video company to outfit and install your sound, lighting and video systems.

I owned an audio-video company and have seen many other companies crush a bar or club owner with an inflated AV bid. They do this by overselling the job with much more equipment than is needed for the venue. I have witnessed multiple sound companies working together and placing one bid incredibly high so the other bid which is still high, but lower by $10,000, is immediately accepted by the owners.

Be careful and get multiple quotes from multiple companies, even if you have to call a distributor directly. You can call them to find a certified dealer in your area: JBL, Crest, Mach, Martin, Highend, Turbo Sound, etc.

You can ask for B stock items, or even C stock, from the distributors and they will carry the same warranty. Make sure that if you are sold new equipment that it is not B stock or C stock and represented as new.

Don't forget that you will need electrical outlets for your sound, lighting and video locations, and that the contractor needs to be aware of this early. It should be on the drawings.

Funny fact: If you use home audio equipment, you do not have to pay ASCAP or BMI fees. If you play prerecorded music, you will be contacted by BMI and ASCAP and need to pay yearly fees to these artist representatives. Beware: They circle like vultures over a fresh kill!

Responsibility: Principals, AV companies
Timeline: bids 2-4 weeks-installation 1-2 weeks max

Point of Sale Cash Register System

The process of choosing and installing your POS system is harder and more labor-intensive than you can believe. Once you have chosen your system, have all principals and management go to the classes provided by the manufacturer's rep.

This system, once fully operational and correctly programmed, will save you much grief during your venue's operation. Like a stepchild, you will curse the system in the beginning but come to love and rely on it in the end.

Many operators underestimate the programming portion of the system and are unprepared for their opening. Designate the bar manager one to two weeks to do nothing but program the system. This should be done at the manufacturer's rep's office where he will have all the help and support needed.

Don't forget that the different options available for this system are vast. For instance, you can access the system via the Internet or have it connected to your security camera. You can keep inventory and track specific beer and liquor sales and trends. As these systems get better, the options that become available will be more and more helpful to daily operations.

This system may be leased to save money or purchased outright.

Don't forget to set up your credit card system. This will be integrated with your POS system. Also, add a phone line attached to a backup modem for credit card transactions, in case your Internet access crashes.
Responsibility: Principals, Management team, POS Company
Timeline: 1 to 3 weeks

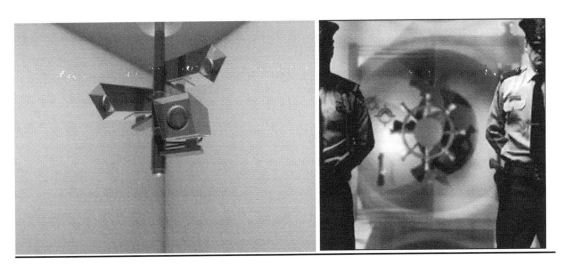

The Wife is not Speaking to Me
One night, this guy comes into a bar and asks the bartender for a drink. Then he asks for another. After a couple more drinks, the bartender gets worried.
"What's the matter?" the bartender asks.
"My wife and I got into a fight," explains the guy, "and now she isn't talking to me for a whole 31 days."
The bartender thinks about this for awhile. "But, isn't it a good thing that she isn't talking to you?" asks the bartender.
"Yeah, except today is the last night."

Recruiting and Hiring Staff

At this point, your management staff will be in place. You should have been handing out job applications to dozens of walk-ups from the day you took over the building and put up your coming-soon sign.

With advertisements in the paper and a now-hiring banner over your door, you can accept all job applications and let people know that the callbacks will be done about one month before opening.

Take a Polaroid picture of every applicant and staple it to the top corner of the application. Also, write notes at the top of every application form. This will help you recall information and your first impressions after meeting applicants.

Staff requirements for your venue will be bartenders, bar backs, busboys, cocktail waitresses, cleaning crew, security, bathroom attendants, DJs, VIP hosts and any other unique needs your venue may require.

Be aware that you may be altering your staff up until the day you open.

Recruiting staff from other venues is known as "head-hunting" in the industry. If you go out to local bars and nightclubs and attempt to hire away their best employees, it is frowned upon but happens often. If you recognize a good employee at another venue, it is okay to introduce yourself and let them know that you are opening a new concept soon. If they show up to fill out an application, then that is great.

Good Internet sites for hiring are MySpace.com classifieds, Craig's List and Auditions.com.
Responsibility: Principals, management team
Timeline: No less than one month from opening, with callbacks to follow within one week

Planning Your Opening Parties

With the information from your contractor and attorney, you should have a good idea now of when you will open.

With this information, look at opening one to two weeks after they say everything will be completed, as things are never on time and always late.

Coordinate with your graphic designer to create invitations with a specific opening date. Also, send advertisements to the local rags, newspapers and magazines.

You and your staff will begin to make contact and guest lists for the upcoming parties.

For the service industry opening party, print 10,000 business-card-style invitations and begin distributing these immediately.

The Little Black Bar Book

Responsibility: Principals, management, graphic designer
Timeline: 1-2 days

Training

Begin training your team members within two weeks of opening. This will include an orientation day, during which all of the team members will meet and greet the management team and principals involved.

Then arrange to go over the training manuals put together by your management team outlining what is to be expected from your team members. The manuals also will cover sensitive information, such as sexual harassment, and oral and written warnings, including suspensions and firing.

Go over all of your policies and procedures. Review the ideas of what the concept is and how you expect the team members to fit into and help define that concept. Outline the standards of service that are expected from every team member.
A few of the items that need addressing:
- **Dress code**
- **Calling in sick**
- **Service standards**
- **Greetings**
- **Legal issues**
- **Expectations**

Set up a day for all of the team members to train on the POS system at the manufacturer's designated location.

Some concepts have different needs and will need longer and more intense training, such as dance routines, table service or bottle-service training. As some team members may have little experience in these areas, longer training may be needed to perfect these skills.

Now is the time to ingrain that this is a family and team. Begin addressing your employees or staff as "team members."
Responsibility: Management team, team members, POS rep
Timeline: 1 week – 1 month

Press Releases

You can hire a public relations firm to help you with this or you can write press releases yourself to be submitted to local news organizations, TV and radio stations, magazines, newspapers and other publications. A PR firm will have established

relationships and contacts to arrange for newspaper, radio and TV interviews. Remember, local and national attention never hurts when gearing up for your big opening.
Responsibility: Principals, PR firm
Timeline: Weeks

Marketing

Getting your name out on the streets and getting people excited about your new concept are the goals of your marketing plan. Now you must create a marketing campaign that stirs people's imaginations and gets them excited and wanting to experience your new concept.

Once again, you have the option of hiring a PR firm to help you with this, or you can put together a marketing campaign using your own in-house resources.

This is the same concept as a getting out the vote campaign; you need to reach out to as many people as possible and spread the word.

Organize staff outings promoting the venue at all of the local hot spots. A good idea is to rent a party bus and load up the staff for a night of partying and promotions.

Flyers, passes, posters, banners and advertisements in the local papers and rags are all powerful tools in marketing your new concept.
Responsibility: Principals, management, team members, PR firm
Timeline: Starting from the time you take over your venue from the landlord

Printing Menus

It's free! Yes, you can get a liquor sponsor to create, print and pay for your drink menu. The liquor company will be more than happy to do this for you, but you will need to put their logo and brand in the menu, along with their product.

The liquor company will supply the graphic designer and the menu sleeves designed to your requests.
Responsibility: Management, liquor company
Timeline: 1 week

Equipment Installation and Dry Goods Delivery

Getting your bar equipment ready to be installed and coordinating with your contractor is a critical path item. The connections and installations need to be made in coordination with the contractor's sub-contractors.

Your dry goods can begin to arrive a week before your opening. Your team members and bar manager will be the ones to inventory, organize, label and stock everything.

Storage areas need to be organized with lots of shelving. Metro racks or tiered storage racks and cages need to be installed before the arrival of your dry goods and liquor.
Responsibility: Management, contractors, team members
Timeline: 1 week before opening

Entertainment and Support Staff

Depending on your concept, you will need to hire DJs, bands, lighting operators, sound engineers and any other unique entertainment your concept may require.

You need to place an advertisement for this. There are so many DJs looking for work that you will have more house, hip-hop and techno demo CDs than you will know what to do with.

Joke: "Why do disc jockeys shorten their names to DJs? Because it is easier to put it on their next job application!"

Hiring a good house band is very difficult and can be costly. Negotiating an agreement with a house band can be done by salary or on a performance-based fee structure, in which they need to have a certain-sized crowd and will get paid a percentage of bar sales or door cover.
Responsibility: Principals, general manager
Timeline: 1 week

Ordering in Your Liquor and Beer

Your bar manager will meet with all of the local distributors and figure out what brands you will carry for your well, call and premium liquors, and the amount of product you will need for your inventory.

This is the time to squeeze your distributors for two-for-one case deals and plenty of free stock for your opening parties. You can ask your distributors to set up meetings with different brand representatives and then ask directly for their support and free product or sponsorship deals.

Negotiating discounts with vendors who are going to directly benefit your concept is a must. If you are a bar that sells high volumes of beer, then you can negotiate between Budweiser and Miller, for example, to see who will give you the most support.

All of your distributors will have credit applications that need to be filled out and sent off for approval.

Your liquor, beer and wine cannot be delivered until your licenses have been approved by the city and are posted in your venue.
Responsibility: Bar manager, principal
Timeline: 1-2 weeks with negotiations

Construction Finals and the Finishing Touches
Your contractor should be calling for inspections for each of the trades in the construction's final phases.
- Electrical
- Plumbing
- Mechanical
- Fire and life safety
- Health

Now that the major construction items are completed, you can begin adding the finishing touches such as art objects, moose heads, paint effects or other décor items.

Industry secret: Once you have gotten your C of O or TCO, have the construction company come back in and add anything that might have been missed.

You can work out a deal with the electricians to come back and add lighting or a few outlets you missed for TVs or a video projector.

Your team members should be willing to help add décor, paint or do just about anything else needed to get the venue ready. Always reward these dedicated team members with better shifts, daily payment and lots of soda and pizza.

This is the reason why you should leave one week of time after the C of O and before opening to the public.

Responsibility: Contractor, team members, principals
Timeline: 1-2 weeks

The Little Black Bar Book

ATM
Have an ATM in your bar or nightclub. The best way to achieve this is to find a local company that will supply the machine, sharing with them the fees charged to your customers on every transaction.

You will need to supply a phone line and power outlet for the machine in your contract with the company that supplies the ATM. Try to get them to pay for the monthly phone line cost.
Responsibility: Management
Timeline: 2-3 days

In-house training of the Team Members and Organizing the Bar
Once you have your C of O or TCO in place, you can bring in your team members to begin a whirlwind of cleaning, stocking, organizing and training over the next few days. These will be the bar's most hectic and crazy times. You will be working 24 hours a day with staff and construction workers getting things organized and in place for your VIP parties and opening.

Getting your team members comfortable and getting the tools in place for them to perform is very important. Make sure certain items such as the POS system is online, and have the team members practice and familiarize themselves with the system. The POS techs will be working out the bugs of the system and training the entire team.

All schedules for the next two weeks for all of the staff should be posted at this time, with a note that reads: *"Team members, shift changes can and will be made on a daily basis, if necessary."*
Responsibility: Management, Liquor Company, Team members
Timeline: 1 week

Final License Approval
Once you have your C of O or TCO, the city will be ready for one final walkthrough before signing off on and issuing your liquor and beer licenses.

Your liquor and beer distributors will be waiting with loaded trucks to drop off your first loads of product.
Responsibility: Attorney, city inspector, liquor license commission, contractor, principals
Timeline: 1 day

Full Team Member Work Days
Now that you have your licenses and your C of O or TCO in place, you can take one to two days and have a mandatory team cleaning and preparation party. Provide pizza and

drinks for all of the team members as they prepare the bar or nightclub for opening and any last-minute details.

Any running around that needs to be done should be done by your team members. Have your management team delegate whatever they need done to the team members under them.

This is the time to CLEAN EVERYTHING! Up until you open, you will be cleaning, stocking, organizing and training.
Responsibility: Principals, team members, management
Timeline: 1-2 days

Systems Testing and Last-Minute 'Oh Shit!' Stuff.
This is the time before you open that you will test every system in the bar. Be sure to check these items out:

- Run toilets and sinks nonstop for an hour;
- Test your drains behind the bar and make sure that the back bar area is water-tight;
- Add thermostats in all of your coolers and freezers full of stock;
- Run your sound system at full volume for as long as you can. You will not be able to set the levels until you have a full bar, as bodies absorb sound;
- Run your intelligent lighting system for more than 8 hours straight;
- Set and mark all of the lighting levels for the club;.
- Test POS system;
- Let your ice machine fill, then empty it and have it fill again. Measure the amount of time it takes to refill. Find the number for an ice-delivery service and place it on your emergency call list in the office;
- Make sure your credit card service works;
- Test your security radios with the sound system set at the operating volume;
- Have a phone list for all of the sub-contractors, along with all of your emergency numbers, on the wall in the office;
- Test your HVAC, especially in the summer;.
- Go to the bank and get as much change as you can afford. You will need it!
- Make all of your banks for your bartenders. Each bank should be between $300 and $500 for each cash drawer for each POS;

- Test your security video system if you have one. Every bar should have a minimum of two cameras, as well as one over the front door and one in the office;
- Have a full team-member meeting to go over any last-minute details.

Responsibility: Principals, Team members, Management
Timeline: 1 day

TIME TO OPEN THE DOORS

Friends and Family Night

This is the first real test of your staff and venue, and here is where you will be able to take notes and make corrections under real working conditions with as little stress as possible.

You should have no more than 100 close friends and relatives at this event. This is a real-life systems check, so you should prepare simple comment cards for your guests. Make sure plenty of pens are available.

Following this event, you will have a full team-member meeting to discuss issues and shortcomings of the staff or venue.

The next day, have your contractor and his sub-contractors ready to handle any issues that arose during the event.
Responsibility: Principals, team members, management
Timeline: 4 hours for the party, 1-2 hours team meeting

Local Press and Media Night with Service Industry Principals

This night is to introduce your concept to the press, media, VIPs and local service-industry principals, such as other bar, nightclub and restaurant in the area.

Everything needs to be right, from the ambiance to, most importantly, the service. All drinks and food will be free. Samples of your specialty drinks and menu items should be served to your guests throughout the night.

Following this event, you will have another full team-member meeting.
Responsibility: Principals, team members, management
Time: 2-4 hours for the party, 1 hour team meeting

The Service Industry VIP Night

The service industry VIP party is your big opening to the general public and should last no more than three to four hour, with free drinks for all of the local service-industry workers, such as bartenders, cocktail waitress, security guards, bar backs, waiters, waitresses and managers from every bar, nightclub and restaurant in the city.

Any locals whom you would consider VIPs for your concept should also be invited. For example, if you are a sports bar, you invite local sports team members.

Following this, you will have another full team-member meeting.
Responsibility: Principals, team members, management
Time: 3-4 hours for the free party, then begin charging for the first time and close your doors at what will be your regular closing time. Followed by a one-hour team meeting.

The Day After
Call for a full team-member meeting, depending on how well things went. If things were a disaster, you need the entire team working quickly to resolve the situations and issues right FU@$!^& now! All of the corrections need to be made before your first weekend opening to the general public.
Responsibility: Principals, Team members, Management
Time: 1-2 hour team meeting

Opening Your Doors to the Public
Congratulations! This is what you have worked so hard for, and all the long hours and capital invested have finally paid off. Here is your concept come to life.

Now, you will finally see what you have created with your first full weekend open to the public. Remember that problems will arise and you will need to stay calm and focused to get through this first weekend.

Try to stay relaxed and your team will take notice of your professionalism. You should be overstaffed for the first few weeks. Try to observe the staff and see who is working well and representing the type of character and spirit you are looking for in your concept.

Allow your management team to make corrections and handle the staff and patrons. This is their responsibility and you need to allow them to work.

Use key team members who perform well as examples to the other team members. This is how you can mold your team and your concept to be one fluid machine.

Burn Money

Let's discuss what burn money is. It is the money that goes out every month that will not contribute to you making a profit or benefiting from in any way in the immediate future. There is no ROI, or return on investment.

Rent is the largest and best example of burn money, as every month this large chunk of cash will go out with no possibility of any kind of ROI.

Insurance is another good example of burn money, along with other expenses such as payroll, salaries, power, water and trash. These are expenses you can count on every month to go out.

Investing in advertising is not burn money as you are expecting a return on investment for every dollar spent.

It is a good idea to have the total amount of burn money for three to six consecutive months of business in the bank when you open any new concept. This will provide a cushion for any unforeseen occurrences.

How do you limit your burn money or make it work for you? If at all possible, buy the venue you are attempting to take over. This will mean the business is paying the note on the property, and any appreciation that is made during the life of the business is added to the bottom line.

Also, find a venue that the owner will contract a lease option to buy. This gives you time to come up with the money from your profits to purchase the building. You must first decide what the fair market value of the property is, then agree that you will have enough time in one or two years to raise the needed capital to purchase the property before the lease option expires.

Final Thoughts

Falling Into the Trap

Once you have successfully opened your first bar or nightclub, then the real test of being a successful owner or operator begins. If the temptations haven't already been too much for you during the hiring period, then the addition of a fully operating venue in its honeymoon period will tip the scales for sure.

Temptations in the business include drugs, alcohol and sex from both staff and patrons, and they can trap even the most ethically sound individuals. I have watched both partners and acquaintances in the business running headlong down dark paths to tragic ends.

The end has come in many forms to many of my friends and acquaintances from drug overdoses, DUIs, suicides and other cruel ends. God rest their souls.

The end for many is not the end of life, but of a way of life that has taken them to the brink and somehow they have been saved through intervention or abandonment. As I have never tried drugs and don't drink, I find it rewarding that I can attend Cocaine Anonymous meetings to help a friend by intervening and supporting them to get clean. I actually end up appreciating the teachings and fundamentals for this drug program because they are great lessons for life in general.

The 12 steps of CA and AA! I still carry a beaten and battered copy of the 12 steps of CA. Is it a talisman for my soul like a Hail Mary when I am asking God for help or just giving thanks for everything I am fortunate enough to have in my life!

Below is the true 12-step program and under that are the 12 steps of being a bar owner.

The True 12 Steps of Alcoholics Anonymous

1. We admit we are powerless over alcohol—that our lives have become unmanageable;
2. We have come to believe that a power greater than ourselves can restore us to sanity;
3. We have made the decision to turn our will and lives over to the care of God as we understand Him;
4. We have made a searching and fearless moral inventory of ourselves;
5. We have admitted to God, ourselves and another human being the exact nature of our wrongs;
6. We are entirely ready to have God remove all of these defects of character;
7. We have humbly asked Him to remove our shortcomings;

8. We have made a list of all the people we have harmed, and are willing to make amends to them all;
9. We will make direct amends to such people wherever possible, except when to do so would injure them or others;
10. We will continue to take personal inventories, and when we are wrong, promptly admit it.
11. We will seek through prayer and meditation to improve our conscious contact with God as we understand Him, praying only for knowledge of His will for us and the power to carry that out;
12. Having had a spiritual awakening as the result of these steps, we will try to carry this message to alcoholics and to practice these principles in all our affairs.

The Truly Deviant 12 Steps of the Bar and Nightclub Business

1. I admit I have power over drugs and alcohol and my live is easily manageable;
2. I believe that drugs and alcohol are not greater than myself and that I can control them, and I need them to maintain my sanity;
3. I have made a decision that I will party like a rock star, and since I am The Man, everything will always be alright;
4. My morals are mine and I'm just too busy now to go searching for anything but another girl;
5. I let everyone know that I can do no wrong and am infallible. And anyone who thinks they can tell me how to run my bar is an idiot;
6. I am entirely ready to have God and all my peers accept that I am The Man;
7. Dear God, please never let the party stop;
8. I must make a list of all the hot girls and cool people I hang out with and call all of them this weekend;
9. I will call and invite all of my old girlfriends, and even people who aren't cool anymore, and I will make them all wait in line and pay cover at my club for the next big event. And if they don't like it, screw them;
10. I will continue to take a personal inventory of all my cool things, such as my cars, my watch and all of my friends. And I will admit that I am rarely ever wrong;
11. I will seek through prayer and meditation to improve my conscious contact with God as I understood Him, praying only for knowledge of His will for me and the power to carry that out;
12. My life is awesome. I have never had more fun, and to hell with stupid people if they can't take a joke. Why doesn't everyone want to be like me? I will keep the party going for anyone who wants to join.

Final Thoughts

"The bar business is truly the fast lane and that would explain why life is one big blur."

The speed and ferocity that the bar business eats patrons and operators alike is not to be blamed on the alcohol or drugs but on the individual's need to experiment with experiences that will soar them to the moon, and then dump them in hell! These highs and lows are what life's memories are made of and no one ever remembers the middle!

Made in the USA